COPTIC ORTHODOX

PATRIARCHATE

See of St. Mark

LIFE OF HOPE

By

H.H. POPE SHENOUDA III

Title	: Life Of Hope.
Author	: H. H. Pope Shenouda III.
Translated By	:Dr. Wedad Abbas.
Illustrated By	: Sister Sawsan.
Typesetting	: Y. M. Ekladios.
Press	:Dar El Tebaa El Kawmia, Cairo.
Edition	: First Edition- July 1999.
Legal Deposit No.	: 9610 / 1999.

H.H. Pope Shenouda III
117th Pope and Patriarch of Alexandria and the See of St Mark

Table of Contents

	Page
Introduction	7
Chapter 1	
Hope	9
Chapter 2	
All things work together for good	23
Chapter 3	
Come to Me, all you who labor and are heavy laden, and I will give you rest	35
Chapter 4	
God wants our salvation	47
Chapter 5	
God's care for the little things	67
Chapter 6	
God the loving and compassionate	91
Chapter 7	
"I am with you and will keep you wherever you go, and will bring you back to this land"	101
Chapter 8	
Without Asking	115
Chapter 9	
God's Hand With Us	133
Chapter 10	
Wait For The Lord	143

	Page

Chapter 11
    "Comfort the fainthearted, Uphold the weak"   155

Chapter 12
    God takes the initiative   165

Chapter 13
    The end of a thing is better than its beginning   177

Chapter 14
    You can do everything No purpose of yours can be withheld from you   183

Chapter 15
    Behold, a door standing open in heaven   193

The Story of This Book

Many are those in need of a word to restore to them hope, in need of a window that brings in light to disperse the darkness overwhelming them.

Such people become mean-spirited when facing problems which seem complicated and not easy to solve, and fears of not having them solved give the devils opportunity to fight them. They imagine they cannot get rid of the sins which dominated over them for long and which they confessed many times without being able to stop them. They say with David the Prophet,

"Many are those who say of me:

There is no help for him in God"(Ps. 3: 2)

They stop at these words and do not complete the words of the psalm which contain hope.

Due to the importance of this subject and the need of many to hear about hope, I included it in innumerable sermons. Thus it was difficult to print a book containing all the material delivered on the topic "hope".

However, I selected fifteen articles to be included in this book till another part is issued or the remainder is added in a new edition of the book.

Hope is one of the three main virtues mentioned by St. Paul in (1 Cor. 13: 13), namely: Faith, Hope, Love.

For each of the above virtues we have printed a book, thus forming a series for you.

Pope Shenouda III

CHAPTER 1

HOPE

Hope is one of the three main virtues mentioned by St. Paul the apostle in his first epistle to the Corinthians; he said, "... *faith, hope, love, these three ..*" (1 Cor. 13: 13). These three virtues are connected because faith brings forth hope, as the person who believed in God usually has hope in Him, and who has hope in God loves Him, thus attaining the utmost relationship with God in love.

Hope is as ancient as humanity and even more ancient.

The first hope humans had was the hope of salvation when the Lord God promised Adam and Eve that the woman's seed will bruise the serpent's head (Gen. 3: 15).

This hope filled their hearts thousands of years till it was realized in the Lord's Incarnation and Crucifixion for mankind. Even those who did not receive this hope, lived it as St. Paul said, "*not having received the promises, but having seen them afar off were assured of them*" (Heb. 11: 13). So, they died in faith until God sought them and brought them back to Paradise.

Hope existed even before Adam and Eve in the history of the first creation.

There was hope for that formless void earth overwhelmed by darkness and waters (Gen. 1: 1). And God realized that hope for the earth when He said "*Let there be light*", and there was light. Then God adorned the earth with trees, flowers, fruits and birds till it became in the most beautiful form, and God saw everything was very good. Therefore, though the earth be, at any time, void and formless or covered with waters and darkness, there is still hope that God brings out of all this such beautiful nature that we see today.

Hope is an important thing in life, and if one loses hope, one will lose everything.

A person who loses hope falls in despair and distress, in mean- spiritedness, in anxiety, confusion and aimless expectation, and may thus become a plaything in the hand of Satan. That is why we say that it is Satan who leads to despair.

However, God's children always have hope and live in hope all the time. In affliction they have hope, and whenever all matters become complicated or God seems to tarry and everything looks dark, there is hope still.

God's children have hope also in eternal life.

In eternity, God's promise will be realized concerning what eye has not seen, nor ear heard, nor have entered into the heart of man. It is the eternal life which we struggle here on the earth to attain as St. Paul the apostle says, "*If in this life only we have hope in Christ, we are of all men the most pitiable*" (1 Cor. 15: 19). There is also hope in repentance for sinners. Even the most wicked sinners on the earth have hope.

There was hope for the thief on the cross in the most serious hours of his life.

There was hope also for Zacchaeus the chief tax collector who represented maximum oppression in his time, and for the Magdalene woman who had seven devils and became one of the saintly Marys and even deserved to announce the Resurrection of the Lord to the eleven disciples. There was hope even for the fruitless tree which gave no fruit for three years, as the Lord said, "*I dig around it and fertilize it. And if it bears fruit, well.*" (Lk. 13: 8,9).

Christianity gives hope even to the bruised reed and smoking flax.

God is able to bind up the bruised reed, and to the smoking flax send a wind to kindle it. Therefore, to give hope, God said, *"Comfort the fainthearted"*. He gave hope even to the weak hands and the feeble knees (Isa. 35: 3).

In Christianity there is hope to everybody; to individuals, to organizations, to churches, to countries, and to the whole world.

We have hope that God seeks humanity at all times. This hope within the believers never weakens -even though matters sometimes seem hard. How can that be?

Jonah the Prophet had hope when he was in the belly of the fish.

It is possible for someone to have hope while in a fish's belly? Yes, Jonah knelt and prayed to the Lord God from the fish's belly, and said, *"Yet I will look again toward Your holy temple"* (Jon. 2: 4). He had hope, and his hope was realized.

There was hope for three young men in the fiery furnace and for Daniel in the lion's den.

There was hope for the barren woman who had not borne. The Lord said to such a woman in the Book of Isaiah, *"Sing, O barren ... Enlarge the place of your tent ... your descendants will inherit the nations, and make the desolate cities inhabited"* (Isa. 54: 1-3).

There was hope for the dead who were raised as a symbol for us. Even Lazarus who was dead for four days and there was a stench as his sister Martha said (Jn. 11), was raised by the Lord giving us hope.

There was hope in healing the incurable diseases.

The Lord gave sight to the blind and health to the mame, the paralyzed and crippled, to the disabled and to the withered hand.

Even the man who spent thirty-eight years waiting beside the pool for someone to put him into the pool when the angel stirred up the water, this man had his hope realized and the Lord Christ came and said to him, "*Rise, take up your bed and walk*" (Jn. 5).

Even though the matter seems impossible, hard or complicated, there is hope offered by God. The Lord gave us a beautiful example when He said, "*With me it is impossible, but not with God; for with God all things are possible*"(Mk. 10: 27). Deeper words also He said, "*all things are possible to him who believes*"(Mk. 9: 23).

The words "*all things are possible*" give us limitless hope.

St. Paul said in hope, "*I can do all things in Christ who strengthens me*"(Phil. 4: 13). The expression "*all things*" is a very wide expression which gives an idea about the unlimitedness of hope due to the unlimitedness of God's power and love.

In Christianity, hope is limitless, and a Christian can test himself, whether he has the virtue of hope or not, when he falls in trouble or in various afflictions, in sufferings, or in problems which seem to have no solutions, he feels through hope that God has many solutions and that He will certainly come even though people think He is late.

Believe me, sometimes I blame our father and teacher David the prophet for his words to God, "*hasten, do not delay*".

My brothers, God does not hasten nor linger. God works, all the time, and does not delay even though the disciples thought that the fourth watch passed without His coming. He will certainly come if we have faith. We should believe that God will act, powerfully, and He will act in the proper time.

As for the word "delay", it has a relative meaning to humans. They think God delays, but in fact He fulfills His promises which are given by His wisdom according to His true look to everything as in reality.

God works all the time even if we think at any time that He has delayed. The Psalmist says, "*Wait on the Lord. Be of good courage, and He shall strengthen your heart. Wait, I say, on the Lord!*"(Ps. 27: 14).

But what is the real meaning of hope?

One hopes in God and waits on Him but not with anxiety, impatience, grumbling, or doubt.

One should wait for and on the Lord with a strong heart, strengthened with faith that God works. We do not say that God will work; this is a low level, but one should have hope that God works actually.

You should trust, not that God will work in the future, but, that He works now. This will give you hope in what you do not see of God's work but trust He is doing. An aeroplane seems-to a person who uses it for the first time-standing still in the air whereas it is actually flying at more than 800 kms/hour! Some of the plane's propellers -as well as many other parts- seem as if not moving while they are working at a very high speed.

God works. You may not see that but you believe in it, and consequently, you will have hope in the result of that work which you will see afterwards.

In afflictions, one who has hope in God, will benefit from the words of the psalm, "*Though an army encamp against me, my heart shall not fear. Though war may rise against me, in this I will be confident*"(Ps. 27: 3).

This confidence is due to having hope in God's work. It makes one see, as Elisha saw, that God's army is surrounding the city, and that *"those who are with us are more than those who are with them"*(2 Kgs. 6: 16). Thus, one says with the psalmist, *"Our soul has escaped as a bird from the snare of the fowlers. The snare is broken, and we have escaped"*(Ps. 124: 7).

A person having hope, will not see afflictions, but will see God who overcomes such afflictions.

The Lord said "I have overcome the world". Therefore, one should have this hope to the end of one's life, all the time, and in every case and situation. One should not quit hope, for hope gives peace of heart, confidence and joy as the apostle says in the Epistle to the Romans *"rejoicing in hope"*(Rom. 12: 12).

We should have hope that God can do everything, and that no purpose of His can be withheld from Him. We should have hope in God's love and promises.

We should have hope in Him who said, *"I will not leave you nor forsake you"*(Josh. 1: 5), *"I am with you always, even to the end of the age"*(Mt. 28: 20), *"I have inscribed you on the palms of My hands"*(Isa. 49: 16), and who said also, *"the gates of Hades shall not prevail against it"*(Mt. 16: 18). We should have hope in God who worked in the olden times and who works all the time, to whom we ought to say as they said in the past, *"Let God arise, let His enemies be scattered, let those who hate Him flee before Him."*

We hope that God who conquered the world will conquer it again, will conquer atheism and overcome permissiveness and materialism, He will overcome malice, hatred, division, dessolution, and violence prevailing in the world.

This is the God in whom we hope, who will restore to the world its original form, who always supports His children, whom St., John saw in the Revelation in the midst of the seven lamp-stands with the angels of the seven churches in His right hand (Rev. 1: 13-20).

God is still in the midst of His children, and the angels and leaders of the churches are in His right hand. He sings His beautiful song, *"no one is able to snatch them (My sheep) out of My Father's hand"* (Jn. 10: 29).

We have hope in God of whom St. John the beloved said in his Revelation, *"I looked, and behold, a door standing open in heaven"*(Rev. 4: 1). It is true that a person who lives with hope always finds a door open in heaven, and sees God standing at that door and saying that He opens and no one shuts (Rev. 3: 7).

God is concerned about our salvation more than we are, and loves us more than we love ourselves. He knows what is good for us more than we do. He is the Almighty who leads the whole universe and holds the life of all people in His hands. He manages everything according to His unlimited wisdom. Therefore, we have hope in this God, and we sing with the apostle:

"All things work together for good to those who love God" (Rom. 8: 28).

The good meant here is not the good as we understand it, but the good according to the divine measures. It is this Beneficent God in whom we put our hope, to whom we say in some prayers of the Holy Mass, *"the hope of those who are helpless and the help of those who have no helper"*, and in psalm (118: 8) we say *"It is better to trust in the Lord than to put confidence in man. It is better to trust in the Lord than to put confidence in princes"*.

The hope meant is the hope in God's true promises, in

the beautiful eternal life and in the happy resurrection.

It is hope not in the worldly matters, but in the heavenly homeland, "*the city which has foundations, whose builder and maker is God*"(Heb. 11: 10).

Such hope involves belief in another new life void of sin and transgression, belief in the wonderful renewal which will be obtained in heaven when we shall restore our former divine image and be in a state in which we may not sin afterwards but live in the freedom we have from the Lord, which freedom does good only and knows no more sin. It is belief in God's kingdom in which we will live forever, and for which we prepare ourselves now.

The true hope is that by which we hope in things not seen, in things we wait for patiently as the prophet tells us. To that hope we should call all people.

We should say to everyone that every closed door has thousand keys.

God is able to open all closed doors. Every darkness is certainly followed by light, and every problem has a solution or dozens of solutions. Every tribulation is controlled by God, our good God who brings something sweet out of the strong, and something to eat out of the eater. God turns everything to good. Any good thing in our lives comes to us good, and the evil things are turned by God the Beneficent into good.

We, therefore, live in hope and in continuous joy. Peace fills our hearts because we rely on God who does everything good, not on ourselves or on worldly means.

Would that all of us live in this hope as a church seeking and waiting God's Kingdom, hoping for His work in it all the time and believing in His work. Would that all of us live in this hope as a large world with all its continents wishing that God makes peace and good prevails everywhere and love returns to the hearts that people may be attached to God and live in Him as the Lord Christ said, *"By this all will know that you are My disciples, if you have love for one another."* (Jn. 13: 35).

If we do not have such hope, let us ask for it as a free gift from God who fills the hearts with His peace and hope. Glory be to Him forever and ever, amen.

The life of hope needs trust:

The life of hope needs trust in God, in His promises, in His work, in His love to all people, and in His wise dispensation.

To have your heart filled with hope you should trust that God loves you more than you love yourself and that He knows what is good for you more than you know by far. Trust that all God's dispensation for you is out of deep wisdom and goodness even though you are convinced of the opposite.

You should be aware that you are in God's hands alone, not in the hands of the people or in the hands of the devils, or subject to temptations and events.

You are in God's hands, and God has inscribed you on the palms of His hands (Isa. 49: 16). He gives you refuge under His wings (Ps. 90). He keeps you day and night, and preserves your going out and your coming in (Ps. 121). Because He loves you, He called you His child (1 Jn. 3: 1). He is the Shepherd who leads you and you shall not want (Ps. 23: 1). We all are God's people and sheep of His pasture, therefore, as a good shepherd

He cannot neglect His sheep, and as a father He cannot neglect His children.

If you have a problem, you will be in comfort if you wait the Lord; He will save you. Follow the advice given by the psalmist *"Wait on the Lord; be of good courage, and He shall strengthen your heart; wait, I say, on the Lord!"*(Ps. 26(27)).

The advice given by the psalmist is not merely to wait the Lord but to be strong within while waiting.

Do not be troubled or weary while waiting for the Lord, or keep grumbling or protesting: Why have not the Lord worked until now? Where is His love? Where is His work? Let us not wait in doubt of God's work or of the effectiveness of prayers! Let us not wait with inner weakness, low or mean-spiritedness! Nay, all such feelings are against the virtue of hope. A person feeling confusion, despair or fear, or is broken down is a person who has lost hope, whereas a person who waits the Lord in hope, is given power by such hope as Isaiah the Prophet said:

"But those who wait on the Lord shall renew their strength; they shall mount up with wings like eagles, they shall run and not be weary, they shall walk and not faint"(Isa. 40: 31).

What does it mean *"they shall renew their strength"*? It means that whenever the devil fights them with weakness and confusion their strength is renewed when they remember God's true promises and divine attributes, for He is the Father and the Shepherd who keeps, preserves, and helps. He is the compassionate God, the loving, and the beneficent who never sleeps or forgets. Whenever they remember any of these attributes, strength is renewed within them and they mount up with wings like eagles.

Those who wait on the Lord have unlimited trust in God's sublime love to humans, and in God's wisdom which is

beyond our human understanding.

They trust that God always gives even though we do not ask and before we ask, how much rather if we ask. They trust that God gives what is useful not what we ask for exactly, because what we ask for may be unuseful. This shows God's wisdom and love.

Therefore, in the life of hope, you should have trust in God's wisdom managing your life.

Do not insist on your request, but say "Let Your will be done" Say it joyfully, without pain or sadness.

Many things are not known to us, but are known and revealed to God.

Perhaps what you ask for is not suitable or useful to you, or the time is not suitable and God Knows that well and prefers to postpone His response. Be humble then, and let God's wisdom take the action. Wait for the Lord in confidence.

How shameful it is to trust our intelligence and wisdom more than we trust God!

We put solutions, trusting that they are the best or the only good solutions. But God may have another solution that never occurred to our minds, and which is far better than anything we think of. Would that we trust God and wait for His solutions in hope!

Things that help creating trust:

As we trust God's love and wisdom, we should also trust His promises which are full of hope.

We trust His true promises, "*I am with you always, even to the end of the age*"(Mt. 28: 20); "*do not fear, for I am with you*"(Gen. 26: 24); "*I will not leave you nor forsake you. Be strong and of good courage*" "*No man shall be able to stand before you all the days of your life*"(Josh. 1: 5, 6); "*Be strong and of good courage; do not be afraid, nor be dismayed, for the Lord your God is with you wherever you go*"(Josh. 1: 9); "*do not fear, little flock*"(Lk. 12: 32); "*I am with you, and no one will attack you to hurt you*"(Acts 18: 10); "*They will fight against you, but they shall not prevail against you. For I am with you, says the Lord, to deliver you*"(Jer. 1: 19).

So many are the words of hope in the psalms as well.

Would that you collect these verses and read or remember them whenever you are in need of hope in your life. Suffice that you remember the psalm 90 (91) or 120 (121) where the divine inspiration says, "*A thousand may fall at your side, and ten thousand at your right hand; but it shall not come near you. Only with your eyes shall you look, and see the reward of the wicked*", "*For He shall give His angels charge over you, to keep you in all your ways*", "*You shall tread upon the lion and the cobra. The young lion and the serpent you shall trample underfoot. Because he has set his love upon Me, therefore I will deliver him. I will set him on high, because he has known My name*"(Ps. 91). "*He will not allow your foot to be moved ... The Lord is your keeper*", "*The Lord shall preserve you from all evil. He shall preserve your soul. The Lord shall preserve your going out and your coming in ...*"(Ps. 121).

All these verses create hope within oneself and strengthen the heart within.

Hope increases in you when you remember God's dealings with His saints. If you remember all this, your heart will be filled with help, and you will wait the Lord in trust.

CHAPTER 2

ALL THINGS WORK TOGETHER FOR GOOD

Many people fall in severe distress under the pressure of temptations and afflictions, and may even fall in despair, but the Holy Bible comforts them, saying:

"**All things work together for good to those who love God**" **(Rom. 8: 28).**

In fact the Holy Bible is full of many comforting stories in this regard.

The Story of Joseph the Righteous:

Joseph was a person who received harsh treatment from his brothers to the extent that they threw him in a well and sold him to some Ismaelite merchants. And in his master's house though he was very faithful to his master and very successful in his work, a bad accusation was made against him from his master's wife and he was cast in prison for a long time. However, all things worked together for good.

But for the accusation that led to the imprisonment of Joseph, Pharaoh would not have heard about him and made him his prime minister, the second one in the kingdom.

And but for the cruelty of his brothers, he would not have been in Potiphar's house. But for the fact that Potiphar's wife was a sinner, she would not have lusted for him and accused him falsely, which accusation led to his imprisonment. And but for his imprisonment, he would not have got acquainted to the chief butler of Pharaoh who told Pharaoh of Joseph's power to interpret dreams, and been called and released then entrusted with the Kingdom (Gen. 39- 41).

Unless all this had happened, Joseph's brothers would not have repented, wept and confessed their sin, and love would not have been restored to the family and the family saved from the famine and come together in Egypt.

The problem is that people are so involved in the difficulty that they have no hope that it will turn to good.

People stop at the start point which seems bad or painful and do not see the divine action which turns evil to good, which brings out of the strong something sweet (Jud. 14: 14).

No doubt, the story of Joseph the Righteous is a lesson in hope and shows how all things work together for good.

Another amazing point is:

Adam's sin:

It is a sin which led the world to innumerable calamaties. Through Adam sin entered the world, and death through sin (Rom. 5: 12). However, God, who brings out of the strong something sweet, made all things work together for good.

As a result, we came to know practically how God loves us (Jn. 3: 16), and came to know the blessings of atonement and redemption.

Had Adam not sinned, he would have stayed in Paradise, eating and drinking there, and living with the animals, the birds, and the fish. But now, we gained the Kingdom with all its invisible blessings, things which eye has not seen, nor ear heard, nor have entered into the heart of man (1 Cor. 2: 9), where we will be in the company of the holy angels.

This reminds us of another point:

Death:

All people hate death and see in it a cause of distress! People usually put on black clothes because of death and face it with tears and crying. However, even death is a matter which works for good.

Death is a way to a better life, and to a higher level which humanity attains through it.

In the resurrection, we shall be raised in celestial spiritual bodies. We shall be raised in glory in heavenly bodies that can inherit the Kingdom (1 Cor. 15). But for such death, we would continue in that natural body. Does not death also work for good!

Let us contemplate on the story of St. Anthony and the death of his father.

The death of his father was a deep lesson to him in the mortality and futility of the worldly life. Young Anthony looked at his dead father and said, 'where is your greatness and power? You left the world against your will, but I will leave the world wilfully, before they bring me out of it against my will' And this was the beginning of his monastic life.

Diseases:

Disease is a pest which people fight and flee from by medicine and treatment. Yet, disease "*work together for good to those who love God*"(Rom. 8: 28).

Many diseases led to repentance and did what the deepest sermons could not do.

Serious and painful diseases in particular caused so many people to give God promises, to make vows, and to lead a new life with God, or led them to repent and be ready for death. Thus diseases worked for good in such cases.

Other diseases led people to prayer and to fasting.

Diseases led people to visit the holy places, to ask for the intercession of the angels and the saints, to celebrate holy

Masses, and to do charity to the poor and the miserable. In this way, as the sick person benefits from becoming more attached to God, so also his relatives and friends benefit spiritually.

Diseases were useful even to saints, as they made the saints aware of their weakness and delivered them from vain glory.

St. Paul the apostle, recognizing this, says, "*And lest I should be exalted above measure by the abundance of the revelations, a thorn in the flesh was given to me, a messenger of Satan to buffet me, lest I be exalted above measure*" (2 Cor. 12: 7).

St. Paul pleaded with the Lord three times concerning this disease that it might depart from him but the Lord said to him, "*My grace is sufficient for you*". The thorn continued with St. Paul because God -blessed be His name- knows how such a thorn works for good with His saints, giving them humility of heart.

This story of St. Paul's disease reminds us of Jacob the father of fathers.

Jacob struggled with God and prevailed (Gen. 32: 28). He gained blessing, but God touched the socket of his hip, and the socket was out of joint and he limped on his hip (Gen. 32: 25. 31). This disease continued with father Jacob as a gift from God, working with him for good, giving him humbleness that he might feel his weakness lest his heart should have been exalted because of the blessing and of prevailing in his struggle with God.

Job tempted:

One may ask why such a saintly person like Job to whom God testified twice that: "*there is none like him on the earth, a blameless and upright man"*(Job 1: 8, 2: 3), why such a person be subject to temptation!

In fact, this temptation was for good from many aspects:

It was for Job's good; it led him to humbleness.

Job was fought to some extent by vain glory. He was righteous, and he knew this fact about himself as he said, *"I put on righteousness, and it clothed me. My justice was like a robe and a turban"*(Job 29: 14). It was said that he was righteous in his own eyes (Job 32: 1). Thus the temptation was necessary for him, it worked good for him and led him to humility of heart and to God's knowledge. Only when he said, *"I abhor myself and repent in dust and ashes"* (Job 42: 6) God removed the temptation from him.

The temptation was useful to Job's three friends.

Job's friends were miserable comforters (Job 16: 2); they condemned Job (Job 32: 3), they even did not speak of God what is right, and they had to offer for themselves a burnt offering (Job 42: 8).

The temptation was useful to the whole world.

The people learnt from Job's temptation a lesson in patience as St. James the Apostle said, *"My brethren, take the prophets ... as an example of suffering and patience ... Indeed we count them blessed who endure. You have heard of the perseverance of Job and seen the end intended by the Lord ... "* (Jas. 5: 10, 11).

The temptation was even useful to Job himself with regard to his family and property.

"The Lord restored Job's losses ... Indeed the Lord gave Job twice as much as he had before ... Now the Lord blessed the latter days of Job more than his beginning"(Job 42: 10, 12).

And the Lord gave Job sons and daughters, and, *"In all the land were found no women so beautiful as the daughters of*

Job"(Job 42: 15). God gave Job also a long life, "*After this Job lived one hundred and forty years, and saw his children and grandchildren for four generations*"(Job 42: 16).

The temptation was thus for Job's benefit as he endured.

On the other hand, the temptation was a disgrace to the devil.

It was a new defeat for the devil, because he does not feel ashamed because of his sins. So, it was a disgrace to him.

This is how the temptation worked for the good of all parties.

Temptations in general:

Some people fear temptations and get disturbed, but the apostle says,

"My brethren, count it all joy when you fall into various trials"(Jas. 1: 2).

We need to have trust in God's work with us during the temptation and trust that He changes it to good. St. James does not only call us to have patience, but also to feel joy. This brings us to a life of perpetual joy both in grace and in trials. We should say:

The bitter which the Lord chooses for me is better than the honey I chose for myself.

We should say: All your ways, O Lord, are wisely planned, all for good.

Herod wanted to kill Christ while still a child, but this turned to good for Egypt when Christ visited it.

The Lord blessed the hand of Egypt and we gained holy places in it. The idols fell (Isa. 19: 19-22), and when the holy family was dismissed from one city because of the destruction of the idols, the family came to another city in Egypt. Thus many cities were sanctified by the visit of the holy family to our country Egypt. This was also a step towards spreading Christian faith throughout Egypt.

We remember this, happy with whatever happens to us, confident that:

Though the matter be not good in itself, its consequence will certainly be.

Take for example the troubles of David because of King Saul. David was chased by him from one city to another and from one wilderness to the other, he lived as a fugitive in the wilderness and desert with death lying in wait for him in every step. But all this trouble made him ready to shoulder the responsibilities of the kingdom afterwards, for he became more mature, more valiant and enduring. He knew how to wait for the Lord in faith, trusting that He will interfere.

The tribulations he endured became a source for his psalms.

Those psalms David sang accompanied by the lute, the cithara and the flute, and became a fountain of spiritual contemplations and deep prayers for the following generations where request is mixed with thanksgiving and faith. David set for us the way we should follow in prayers while in time of passion and affliction. David became a man of prayer, one (polished) by the temptations. He gained experience through his communion with God.

Had David lived coddled, how his personality would have been!

If afflictions do not work for good on the earth, at least they will prepare for us crowns which the Just Judge will give us on that Day.

Afflictions are a school for prayers.

A comfortable life may lead us astray from God, but a life of pain brings us nearer to God and our prayers become deeper and more frequent and spiritual. We become more attached to God through repentance and reconciliation with Him.

The tribulation in which Joseph's brothers fell made them remember their sin against him *"They said to one another, 'We are truly guilty concerning our brother, for we saw the anguish of his soul when he pleaded with us, and we would not hear; therefore this distress has come upon us ... Therefore behold, his blood is now required of us'"* (Gen. 42: 21, 22).

Even the falling in sin turns, through repentance, to good for the sinner.

Augustine lived in sin for long, and his mother St. Monica wept for him all that time. Then Augustine repented, and the fruit was his wonderful book "Confessions", a spiritual treasure of spiritual benefit to millions of people, through which one knows how to confess publicly, even of the sins one did when child or infant.

The same applies to the sin of David the Prophet.

The sin caused him a state of self-humiliation that he said, *"All night I make my bed swim; I drench my couch with my tears"* (Ps. 6: 6). He confessed to the Lord, saying, *"Against You, You only, have I sinned, and done this evil in Your sight ... Create in me a clean heart, O God, and renew a steadfast spirit within me"* (Ps. 51:4, 10).

This psalm of repentance, as well as other psalms, contained similar feelings of humiliation and contrition.

David was a great king, respectable and honored by all people, but sin humiliated him, so he said:

"It is good for me that I have been afflicted, that I may learn Your statutes"(Ps. 119: 71).

And when David was badly cursed and insulted by Shimei the son of Gera while he was fleeing from Absalom, he did not permit his followers to take revenge from that person but said in humbleness, *"let him curse, because the Lord has said to him, 'Curse David'. ... It may be that the Lord will look on my affliction"* (2 Sam. 16: 10, 12).

How useful likewise was the sin and the punishment for the sinner of Corinth!

The sin and the punishment caused him to mourn and weep sadly, so St. Paul the Apostle, in his Second Epistle to the Corinthians, ordered them to comfort him *"lest perhaps such a one be swallowed up with too much sorrow"*(2 Cor. 2: 7). But it was a lesson to others and to the whole city that they put away from themselves the evil person (1 Cor. 5: 13).

When one falls in sin, this makes him have compassion on those who fall.

The fall makes one aware -by experience- of the strength of the devil's wars and the possibility of falling in sin, because sin *"has cast down many wounded and all who were slain by her were strong men"*(Prov. 7: 26). Therefore St. Paul the apostle says, *"Remember the prisoners as if chained with them -those who are mistreated- since you yourselves are in the body also"* (Heb. 13: 3).

The fall reveals one's nature and weakness.

This turns to good because it makes one more careful and precise in future and makes him keep away from slackness. Likewise, discovering one's weakness gives a chance for rejecting any thought of pride or arrogance that may fight a person afterwards.

You should therefore live in cheerfulness and happiness.

"*Rejoice in the Lord always*" (Phil. 4: 4).

Whatever happens to you, say: We are under the care of God the lover -of- mankind who loves us more than we love ourselves, and who knows what is good for us more than we ourselves know ... He is God who makes everything turn to good for us ... who makes even the laws of nature work together for good ... who created the animals, the birds, and the plants for our good ... who made the air, the sun, the moon, and the stars for us ... who made all thing work together for good, for our comfort and happiness.

Let us give thanks to God who made all things work together for good, for our sake.

God the Benevolent sent His angels to serve us, "*Are they not all ministering spirits sent forth to minister for those who will inherit salvation?*" (Heb. 1: 14). For us, the Lord-Christ set orders in His church, "*And He Himself gave some to be apostles, some prophets, some evangelists, and some pastors and teachers, for the equipping of the saints for the work of ministry, for the edifying of the body of Christ*"(Eph. 4: 11, 12).

Be joyful whatever happens to you, and say: It is all for good.

In this way the man of God becomes free from any psychological diseases, any distress, any disturbance, any sadness, any complexity, and any despair. He will have always a peaceful heart where peace reigns based upon belief in God and His work.

However, all this depends on a condition mentioned in the verse, "*all things work together for good to those who love God*" (Rom. 8: 28).

The condition is to love God.

For some people the afflictions do not turn to good, but perhaps to complaint, trouble, blaspheming and despair.

Some people do not have that love which makes them trust God and trust His promises, His interference, and His presence. Such people do not have enough faith, so they are pressed by the affliction and become confused and troubled; they live the dread of the problem not looking forward for its solution.

Words on Hope

- Would that we do not look at the troublesome present we live, but look with an eye of hope to the joyful future that is in God's land.
- Every problem that looks complex for us, have many solutions with God. And every closed door, has not only one, but rather many keys in God's hand, who opens and no one shuts (Rev. 3: 7).
- Hope prevents fear, anxiety, and confusion, and gives comfort. We even rejoice in hope (Rom. 12: 12).
- Do not look solely at the troubles without God's action who is able to turn evil into good.
- God is able to turn all occurences the direction He wills.
- That which cannot be done by the human weakness, can be done by God's power. And what people's wisdom cannot face, God's wisdom can.
- Be sure that you are not alone, for you are surrounded by the divine help. You are surrounded by heavenly hosts, and the saints intercede for you.

CHAPTER 3

Come to Me, all you who labor and are heavy laden, and I will give you rest

(Mt. 11: 28)

Everyone in this world has certain troubles, whether these are known to others or hidden within oneself, whether they are spiritual, psychological, physical troubles, or family or social troubles.

The Lord Christ came for those in trouble.

He came "*to save that which was lost*"(Mt. 18: 11) ... He came to save the world from sin as Isaiah the prophet says, "*All we like sheep have gone astray; we have turned, everyone, to his own way; and the Lord has laid on Him the iniquity of us all*"(Isa. 53: 6) ... He came to save the world from suffering and troubles as the same prophet says, "*Surely He has borne our griefs and carried our sorrows*"(Isa. 53: 4) ... The Lord Christ Himself says, "*Come to Me, all you who labor and are heavy laden, and I will give you rest*"(Mt. 11: 28).

But why does He say, "*you who ... are heavy laden*"? Perhaps because the one whose burden is light can endure and keep silent, but whose burden is heavy cannot but say 'O Lord' ...

We should in all cases resort to God, whether our burden is heavy or light. But at least if one is under great pressure because of heavy loads, one will find nothing but the Lord's promise to give him rest.

Come ... and I will give you rest. It is a call and a promise.

It is a call from God, and a promise He gives to a troubled world, heavy laden with problems of all kinds: problems of disruption and wars, problems of housing and supplies, problems of marriage and divorce, problems of extremism and terrorism, problems of corruption and addiction ... etc. But in all these problems the Lord says, "*Come to Me, all you who labor and are heavy laden, and I will give you rest.*"

Here we come to know a beautiful attribute of the Lord: that He is comforter.

He gives comfort to the troubled and the heavy laden. Those who resort to other people in their troubles will be more and more troubled, and sometimes find negligence and carelessness, but whoever comes to the Lord Christ will find comfort and rest. He always gives ... He gives people comfort, calmness, rest, peace and inner confidence ... He removes from people their burdens and carries those burdens of them to give them rest. Those also who have God's image do the same.

The Lord God said, *"Call upon Me in the day of trouble, I will deliver you, and you shall glorify Me"*(Ps. 50: 15)

Some people, when in trouble, are pressed by pain and grief, their minds become troubled, their hearts become heavy and may fall in despair. Such people may perhaps begin to complain or cry, without even thinking of resorting to God or putting before them the words of the Psalm:

"Cast your burden on the Lord, and He shall sustain you"(Ps. 55: 22).

Come then and tell the Lord frankly about your troubles, whether caused by the others' treatment or pressures, their oppression or cruelty, or by suspicions, thoughts, sins, or habits prevailing on you. Trust that the Lord knows your troubles more than you know them, and He wants to save you from all of them. So call Him with hope and trust, putting before you the words of the Psalm:

"May the Lord answer you in the day of trouble. May the name of the God of Jacob defend you"(Ps. 20: 1)

Be sure, the church prays for you at the end of the thanksgiving prayer, [All envy, all temptation, all works of

Satan, all intrigues of the wicked rising up of enemies, visible and invisible; do cast away from us, and from all Your people], and in the prayers of the Holy Mass where the priest mentions all your troubles.

Be sure also, the afflictions are not a kind of forsaking.

God permitted that His apostles and saints be afflicted, but He was beside them, comforting them. That is why St. Paul the apostle said about himself and his companions in the ministry, *"We are hard pressed on every side, yet not crushed; we are perplexed, but not in despair; persecuted, but not forsaken"*(2 Cor. 4: 8,9)

Indeed, many are people's troubles, but Christ is ready to comfort them all.

Troubles may come from the others, but sometimes from oneself as in the case of a person defeated by his lust, his nature, or his habits, or troubled by the thoughts which press on him. Such a person wants to prevail over these matters but is not able; he can find support in the words of the Lord, *"Come to Me, all you who labor and are heavy laden, and I will give you rest"*.

Some persons are troubled by some sin and cannot get rid of it.

Such a person returns to sin after repentance and after repeated confessions. He cannot continue in any spiritual exercises he sets for himself, he tries to force himself to the life of righteousness but still lives in sin. His sins are the same since many years, and his bad nature is the same without any improvement! He is conquered and falling. Sin has almost become a second nature to him, and he has sought the spiritual fathers and guides, and the fathers' sayings and history of saints but with no avail. Such a person has only to seek the Lord who said, *"Come to Me, all you who labor and are heavy laden, and I will give you rest"*.

Failure of seeking other than God:

Why do you keep the Lord to the end? Start rather with Him so that you may attain and be not lost. Listen how the Lord blames us, saying,

"My people ... have forsaken Me, the fountain of living waters, and hewn themselves cisterns-broken cisterns that can hold no water" (Jer. 2: 13)

It is true, many people seek broken cisterns, whether the defect is in the others or in themselves. When one of those faces a problem, he tries to solve it by his own mind and intelligence, by his own tact and planning, or seeks the others' support. He will not benefit from all this because he did not cast his burden on the Lord who shall sustain him. He did not seek Christ to give him rest but tried to depend on an arm of flesh! He neglected the words of the Lord *"Come to Me"*, therefore he fails and finds no solution for his problems.

King Ahab desired the vineyard of Naboth the Jezreelite and sought the counsel of Jezebel instead of the Lord's, and he was lost. He put his troubled head on Jezebel and was lost.

Likewise, Samson put his troubled head on Dalila, and he was lost!

None of them found a solution for his problem, the same as the Jews •who sought Pharaoh to comfort them but he increased their burdens, saying, *"You are idle! Idle!"* (Ex. 5: 17). And when the people went to Rehoboam to make the yoke his father Solomon put on them lighter, he answered them, *"my father chastised you with whips, but I will chastise you with scourges!"* (Kgs. 12: 14).

The arm of flesh cannot save man, but it is God who saves.

Therefore lift your eyes to God and say to Him: I'll cast all my burden on You and will think of it no more. It is You who will find solution for my problem, for it is You alone who has solutions. Whenever I seek others, my problems get more complexed and increase.

It is strange indeed that some people try to solve their problems by sins!

Some people try to solve their problems by lying, and sometimes claim that it is not a serious lie (a white lie)! Some others behave deceitfully and cunningly or even use violence. Some may escape from facing the problem by wine, drugs, sedatives, narcotics or smoking, and none of these solves the problems but adds to it. Some may go even further by seeking magicians, fortune tellers or swindlers, but with the same result.

Some others try to solve their problems by imagination or day dreams.

Such people imagine that they have become so and so, even to enjoy imagining, if not to realize it! That is what they say to themselves, 'If I wake up from my dreams, I will sleep again to have the same dreams!' But the day dreams do not solve one's problems which remain unsolved; they are only solved by the Lord who says, "*Come to Me ... and I will give you rest*".

God alone have solutions for the problems:

Some persons could find no solution except in God, such as the three lads in the furnace of fire, Jonah the Prophet in the belly of the fish, and Daniel the Prophet in the den of the lions. Indeed who could have the power to save all of them except God alone? He sent His angel and shut the lions' mouths (Da. 6:

22), He ordered the fish to vomit Jonah onto a dry land (Jon. 2: 10), and He did not permit the fire to cause harm to the three lads.

God's hand interfered also to solve the Arian problem which faced the church.

It is true that the whole church rose against Arius the heretic, and he was excommunicated by the ecumenical council, and St. Athanasius refuted his ideas, but he continued shaking the people's faith. He even sought the protection of the emperor who ordered that he be accepted. However, the Lord addressed the church, saying, "*Come to Me ... and I will give rest*", thereupon prayers were raised and God responded, for the entrails of Arius quashed out and he died.

God did the same for the army of Sennacherib, and the horsemen of Pharaoh.

When Hezekiah the king tore his clothes, covered himself with sackcloth and went into the house of the Lord casting his burden on Him, the angel of the Lord went out and killed in the camp of the Assyrians one hundred and eighty-five thousand (2 Kgs. 19: 1, 35). The same happened to Pharaoh and his army as they were over thrown by the Lord in the midst of the sea because Moses the prophet sought God and said to the people, "*Stand still, and see the salvation of the Lord ... The Lord will fight for you, and you shall hold your peace*" (Ex. 14: 13, 14).

Indeed, when all solutions fail, God's solution become evident. God fights for you, and you shall hold your peace.

God's promise is honest "*I will give you rest*". These beautiful words are quoted in a song which says, 'When I am in trouble, to whom shall I go but to You'. The same happened in the days of Diocletian as the Lord gave rest to the church and saved it from Diocletian who shed the blood of thousands of martyrs and even more of a whole city among whom were the martyrs of Achmim and Esna. God gave salvation through Constantine who issued the Decree of Milan for religious liberality. God saved His church also from the persecution of Saul of Tarsus, and turned him into St. Paul the most powerful evangelist in Christianity.

We cannot forget also how God saved David the Prophet from king Saul who pursued him in the wilderness.

God's solutions are in fact the strongest and most successful, so we should seek them and hold fast to them.

Jacob the father of fathers was afraid of his brother Esau and of meeting him, but he held to the Lord and said to Him, *"Deliver me, I pray, from the hand of my brother, from the hand of Esau; for I fear him, lest he come and attack me and the mother with the children"*(Gen. 32: 11). So, Esau ran to meet him, and embraced him, and fell on his neck and kissed him, and they wept (Gen. 33: 4). Jacob held also to the Lord who wrestled with him; he said to Him, *"I will not let You go unless You bless me!"*(Gen. 32: 26)

You also, if you could prevail in your struggle with God -like Jacob- He will give you rest and relieve you from all your troubles.

Simon Peter toiled all the night and caught nothing, but when he met the Lord and let down the net at His word, he caught a great number of fish and their net was breaking (Lk. 5: 4-6). And the sinful woman who washed the feet of Christ with her tears and wiped them with her hair could obtain salvation and forgiveness of her sins. This would not have been possible if she had not sought him.

You should come to God, but how?

How should you come to God?

1. Come with a contrite heart as the lost (prodigal) son did:

He was in a bad condition in a far country, but he thought of coming to his father to find rest, and he came with a contrite heart, saying, *"Father, I have sinned against heaven and in your sight, and am no longer worthy to be called your son"* (Lk. 15: 21). This humility made his father welcome him, put the best robe on him and a ring on his hand, and make a great dinner for him, whereas his older brother was lost because he refused to come and spoke haughtily to his father.

Do not come to God haughtily accusing Him of forsaking or persecuting you.

Do not ascribe to God all the causes of your problems, not believing that you are the real cause, but ascribing the cause to being forsaken by God!! Come to Him in humility to reconcile with Him as one of the fathers said:

Reconcile with God, and you will find that both heaven and earth reconcile with you.

So, you should come to God, not only to have rest from your troubles and solution for your problems but first to reconcile with Him; for perhaps the main cause of your problems is that you are not on good terms with God or that your conduct is not pleasing to Him. He says to you, 'I am ready to give you rest, but you should abandon the sinful way you are walking in'. He says also,

" 'Return to Me, and I will return to you', says the Lord of hosts" (Mal. 3: 7)

2. Come then to Him repenting in order to reconcile with Him.

When you reconcile with God, you will find all the world reconciled with you and God will give you comfort and peace of heart. He will give you inner peace, trust and confidence; for in most cases one's troubles are due to an internal cause. Here I remember with admiration the words of St. John Chrysostom:

No one can harm a person unless such a person harms himself.

The cause of your trouble may be the harm you do to yourself, and if you reconcile with God and come to Him repenting, you will get rid of that harm you caused yourself and you will easily find rest.

3. Come to God by faith and prayers.

Many come to God without believing that He will solve their problems! They even pray without feeling that their prayers will bring any fruit. So they continue in trouble because of lack of faith, hope and trust in God.

The Lord Christ said to the sinful repentant woman, "*Your faith has saved you. Go in peace*"(Lk. 7: 50), and to the Leper whom He cleansed, "*Arise, go your way. Your faith has made you well*"(Lk. 17: 19). He said also to the blind man who sat by the road begging, "*Receive your sight, your faith has made you well*"(Lk. 18: 42), and to the two blind men He said, "*According to your faith let it be to you*"(Mt. 9: 29). Therefore come to Him with faith, trusting that He will give you rest and you will have rest.

4. Come to Him carrying His yoke on you.

For He said, "*Take My yoke upon you and learn from Me, for I am gentle and lowly in heart, and you will find rest for your souls*"(Mt. 11: 29). Bear your cross then and follow Him, and if you come to Him when you are facing problems, do not come discontent and grumbling but in submission to His will. Remember the words of the apostle:

"*My brethren, count it all joy when you fall into various trials*"(Jas. 1: 2).

In this way you will not be pressed by any troubles because you have a wholesome heart which no outer pressures could affect. It is fortified by faith and submissiveness and carries the Lord's yoke with joy. The heart is filled with peace, satisfaction and joy even amidst tribulations.

If you do not have this feeling, ask God for it.

We will give you peace as He promised, "*Peace I leave with you, My peace I give to you*"(Jn. 14: 27). And if you have the fruit of the Spirit, "*love, joy, peace*"(Gal. 5: 22), you will always enjoy rest.

5. Go then into the communion of the Holy Spirit and seek the fruit of the Spirit, then come to God and you will find rest.

CHAPTER 4

God Wants Our Salvation

"He desires all men to be saved and to come to the knowledge of the truth"

(1 Tim. 2: 4)

One may lose hope in salvation because one's enemies have revailed against him and he has no power to resist them, whether those enemies were spiritual enemies or people troubling him in this world, and in all this one cries, *"For strangers have risen up against me, and oppressors have sought after my life. They have not set God before them"*(Ps. 54: 3); *"Refuge has failed me; no one cares for my soul"*(Ps. 142: 4). A sinner may also lose hope in repentance, not being able to attain it or undesirous to have it!

However, we say to each of those and the others:

Do not lose hope, for God is keen on your salvation more than you are. He even seeks it as He does since the beginning...

This story of salvation started since the days of our forefathers Adam and Eve. Both of them fell in sin and were subject to death condemnation. Salvation was very necessary to them, and God Himself worked for their salvation.

Neither Adam nor Eve sought salvation but they even escaped from God's face and hid behind the trees!

Their escaping was not a practical way that leads to salvation, but they did not bother at that time for salvation. They were only involved in fear and shame. There is no mention at all that Adam said to God, 'O Lord forgive me. I have sinned against You, blot out my transgressions'. Eve also did not say anything like that. Perhaps such words were not included in their spiritual terminology at that time.

While they were not seeking their own salvation, God was searching for them.

God searched for Adam and Eve in the garden and called Adam, *"Where are you?"*(Gen. 3: 9). God started the talk and encouraged them to talk to reveal to them their sin and the punishment they deserve. Then God gave them the first promise of salvation that the seed of the woman would bruise the head of the serpent (Gen. 3: 15).

Believe me, if God left man to his own free will or to his own power, no one would be saved at all!

But God seeks everyone's salvation as we see in the parable of the lost sheep and the lost coin (Lk. 15).

The sheep was walking its own way not knowing where it is going or where it is, but the good shepherd was careful for its safety, so he discovered its loss. The shepherd searched after it, pursued it in the mountains and valleys till he found it. It was perhaps a surprise to the sheep to find his shepherd in front of it, embracing it kindly and carrying it on his hands joyfully. Indeed what beautiful words are those said by the divine inspiration about the Lord - The Good Shepherd:

"'I will feed My flock, and I will make them lie down,' says the Lord God. 'I will seek what was lost and bring back what was driven away, bind up the broken and strengthen what was sick'"(Ezek. 34: 15, 16).

It is God who seeks and brings back, binds up and strengthens ... All the work is His not ours .. Does this not bring hope?

In the parable of the lost coin we find the same and even more profoundly.

The coin does not have life, mind, intellect, or will. It does not know where it goes when it rolls down or where it stops, nor knows how to return to the purse or pocket of its owner.

The lost coin is a symbol of many like it.

It is a symbol of many people who have no life nor will, and a symbol of triviality. Had the widow lost a hundred pounds of gold it would have been reasonable to search for it, but one coin only taking all this care is a matter which gives place to consideration and gives an example of deep hope:

God works for your salvation even though you seem of not or little worth!

God gave us the parable of the coin so that we may know how valuable is man to Him.

Some may ask what is the value of a small coin that requires such a serious search and such joy and dinner on finding it? All this in fact is a symbol of God's care for one person however little he may be. The parable shows how God works for our salvation even though we do not seek it, and how He rejoices with the angels for our salvation. Are you not better in the sight of God than one lost coin?

Trust that your soul is valuable to God however little or of no value it may seem to other people or to you. See how the Lord sought the salvation of the Samaritan woman who was despised by people, and how He went into the house of Zacchaeus the tax-collector who was considered by all people a sinner and not worthy (Lk. 19: 7)

Indeed, the Lord seeks our salvation and rejoices very much in that.

When He found the lost sheep He laid it on His shoulders rejoicing (Lk. 15: 5), and He says, *"There will be more joy in heaven over one sinner who repents than over ninety nine just persons who needs no repentance"*(Lk. 15: 7). He rejoiced likewise for finding the lost son and offered for him the fatted calf, and for finding the lost coin (Lk. 15: 23, 9). He seeks our salvation than we do ourselves, and rejoices for our salvation than we do. He searches for us more carefully than we seek our eternity. What beautiful words are those said by the apostle about Him:

"He desires all men to be saved and to come to the knowledge of the truth"(1 Tim. 2: 4)

He does not have any pleasure at all that the wicked should die, but that he should turn from his ways and live (Ezek. 18:

23). Therefore in the concluding prayer of each hour we say to Him,

[O Christ ... who does not wish death for the sinner but repentance and life, calling all men to salvation for the promised forthcoming rewards.]

God does not rejoice only at the praising of the Seraphim, the purity of the angels, the preaching of the pastors, or the struggling of the saints, but He rejoices over one sinner who repents more than over ninety nine persons who need no repentance (Lk. 15: 7).

He seeks that which was lost

Do not lose hope if you have gone far astray, because the Lord came to save those who were even lost completely as He said:

"For the Son of Man has come to seek and to save that which was lost"(Lk. 19: 10)

He came to save not only the weak, the sinner, the sick, or the slackening, but to save *"that which was lost"*! Not that which is about to be lost, but who is already lost!! What a great hope to have the Lord coming to seek and to save that which was lost. He did not come to save who asks only for salvation, but it is He Himself who seeks to save everyone.

Even the one who was lost still have hope to be saved!

Yes, certainly Christ came to save the lost; those who are dead in trespasses (Eph. 2: 5)

Do not say then, whatever happens to you or done by you, I am lost; there is no hope in me; there is no way for my salvation! Be sure that even though you are already lost, there is still an open door for your salvation. The Lord came to seek and save that which was lost.

God gave hope to Mary Magdalene who had had seven demons.

St. Mark the Evangelist said that when the Lord rose from the dead, "*He appeared first to Mary Magdalene, out of whom He had cast seven demons*"(Mk. 16: 9). And when He wanted to announce His resurrection to His holy apostles, He chose Mary Magdalene to announce this to them!! We are not certain if she actually had had seven demons, or the number (7) is a symbol of a great countless number of demons!!

However, the past life of Mary Magdalene is forgotten, and she is remembered as the one who announced the Lord's resurrection to the apostles! How amazing! Do you not have hope when you hear the story of this wonderful woman?

Indeed, take heed that you do not despise one of these little ones (Mt. 18: 10)

Do not despise any person, whether such a person is little in age, in spirituality, in character, or having a long sinful past life. Let not any of those be mean-spirited or lose hope.

Believe me, on the Last Day God will give us a different rank than ours in this world.

In this world, our rank is determined according to our age, our position, our talents, or our capabilities. But in eternity the rank will be according to the heart that knows God. Perhaps many of the little ones here, the despised and the disregarded surpass those with talents or holding positions. Therefore do not despise any of these little ones.

When God willed to save Jericho, He chose Rahab the harlot (Josh. 2)

Rahab became one of God's people and is mentioned in the

genealogy of the Lord (Mt. 1). She became a saint, her past forgotten, and she herself a live picture of hope to whoever remembers her.

You may wonder how God cares for a harlot and a woman with seven demons! I tell you it is the same care He gives to the little ones, the despised and the things which are not (1 Cor. 1: 28).

The story of the one (struggling in her own blood) mentioned in the Book of Ezekiel gives hope to all people.

It is written that she was naked and bare, and was thrown out into the open field struggling in her own blood. But did God leave her in this condition? Nay, He said to her, while in this bad condition:

"When I passed by you again and looked upon you, indeed your time was the time of love"

What love do you have, O Lord, for this hateful one, who is naked of any virtue and thrown out in the field? It is true, God loved us while we were sinners. He gave Himself on our behalf, and died for us, the Righteous for the transgressors. And what about that sinful woman? God says, "*I passed by you*" God Himself went to her not waiting her to come. And what else? He says, "*I spread My wing over you and covered your nakedness*". He covered her sin and did not despise her.

'I swore an oath to you and entered into a covenant with you, and you became Mine,' says the Lord God."

In this covenant God gave her many spiritual gifts which He mentioned:

* "*I washed you in water*" i.e. baptism, by which He washed away all her sins.

* "*I anointed you with oil*" i.e. the Myron (Chrismation), by which she got the holy ointment of the Holy Spirit.

* "*I clothed you in embroidered cloth ... I adorned you with ornaments*" i.e. the new righteousness which she got.
* "*You were exceedingly beautiful, and succeeded to royalty*" i.e. to the kingdom.

"*'Your fame went out among the nations because of your beauty, for it was perfect through My splendor which I had bestowed on you,' says the Lord*" (Ezek. 16: 14)

What a wonderful God our kind God is! He bestows His splendor on that who is struggling in her blood and is hated, so she becomes perfect in her beauty, fit for royalty, and enter into a covenant with God, getting His gifts. He even says to her, "*And I put ... a beautiful crown on your head*" (Ezek. 16: 12).

Is not this a wonderful lesson in hope?

It is not important what we have, but what God gives us.

In the story of that sinful woman, which is a symbol of all Jerusalem, God did everything. Had He left her for herself, she would have been lost and would have continued in idol worship. But the goodness of the Lord was moving the conscience continually leading it to repentance. This reminds us of the story of Saul of Tarsus.

The example of Saul of Tarsus

Did Saul of Tarsus seek the Lord Christ, or it was the Lord who sought him?

Saul was a blasphemer, a persecutor, and an insolent man as he said about himself (1 Tim. 1: 13). He used to make havoc of the church, entering every house, and dragging off men and women, committing them to prison (Acts 8: 3). But God was thinking of Saul's salvation and of using his talents for good, so He appeared to him on the way to Damascus and called him.

Saul had not asked for faith, and when he met the Lord he had not arranged for it or even had any idea about it, it never occured to him.

But God sought Saul, saved him, and called him. In fact the conversion of Saul of Tarsus who persecuted the church to be the greatest apostle in Christianity and his labor for the word of God, is a wonderful lesson of hope for all those who are away from God.

One similar to Saul was Irianus the governor of Ansena, and the most violent governor in killing and tormenting the martyrs, but he became himself a martyr by God's work in him and for him.

How God seeks our salvation reminds us of the story of the Virgin of the Song.

The example of the Virgin of the Song:

The Virgin in the Song was asleep after she had taken off her robe, washed her feet and dripped her hands with myrrh, but the voice of her beloved came to her from afar, he came "*leaping upon the mountains, skipping upon the hills*", saying to her, "*Rise up, my love, my fair one, and come away*" (Song 2: 10). He even knocked at her door, saying, "*Open for me, my sister, my love, my dove, my perfect one; for my head is covered with dew, my locks with the drops of the night*"(Song 5: 2). What more could have been done by the Lord in seeking the soul and waiting persistently for her than having His head covered with the drops of the night. It is a lesson in hope for every sleeping soul, not seeking God but only itself and its own comfort!

God Himself is at the door, and is knocking!

He always says, *"Behold, I stand at the door and knock. If anyone hears My voice and opens the door, I will come in to him and dine with him, and he with Me"*(Rev. 3: 20). Our good God did not leave us to our slackening and negligence, keeping away from Him in carelessness.

In His deep love He sought even the tax collectors and sinners; He sat at their banquets to attract them to Himself!

He seeks all those and descends to them to lift them up to Himself. He says about them that they also are the children of Abraham (Lk. 19: 9), and one of the most beautiful verses in this context is the one where He says about Himself that He has come *"to seek and to save that which was lost"*(Lk. 19: 10).

God's care for our salvation is symbolized in the story of the creation.

The first verses of the Book of Genesis say *"The earth was without form, and void"*, and it was covered with waters, and *"darkness was on the face of the deep"* (Gen. 1: 2). A dull picture indeed, but God did not leave the earth like this, *"the Spirit of God was hovering over the face of the waters"*. Then God said *"Let there be light"*, and there was light. God started by organizing the earth, giving it life and beauty, creating trees, flowers and birds, setting the laws of the universe and the solar system: the sun, the moon and the stars, then lastly He created man, thus the earth became beautiful and full of life.

In all this, God gives hope to every void earth filled with waters.

Do not become desperate then even though your soul is fully covered with waters; for the Spirit of God hovers over the face of the waters. And do not become desperate even though the darkness overwhelms you; for the time will certainly come when God will say *"Let there be light"*.

Be hopeful then since God Himself seeks your salvation

The human beings are unable to save themselves. But what they are unable to do for their salvation, God does for them.

It is the story of incarnation and redemption in its deep concept: God Himself seeks the salvation of humanity and offers the atonement and redemption. He also sent the prophets and apostles for this purpose that they may call all people to be reconciled to God (2 Cor. 5: 20). And for the same purpose He sent us the Holy Inspiration in the Holy Scriptures which are able to make us wise for salvation (2 Tim. 3: 15).

Visits of grace to all people:

Visits of grace are to all people not skipping anyone, and even sinners have a portion of these visits!

It is written that He "*went about doing good*"(Acts 10: 38), He searched for the lost souls even though they disobeyed, resisted or fled from Him! He kept after them till He brought them back however desperate was their condition. Here we mention an important rule:

God never becomes desperate of people's salvation even though they themselves became desperate.

God always works; for all people, not only with the person who is spiritually weak, but even with the dead who stank (Jn. 11: 39), with the thief at the last moments of his life (Lk. 23: 43), with Zacchaeus the chief tax collector, even with the Samaritan woman who had five (husbands) (Jn. 4: 18)!!

It was He who looked for that lost woman, to attract her to repentance

He went to the well where that Samaritan woman used to draw water, and arranged wisely for the meeting and the time. He started the talk speaking about the living water, and encouraged her to confess. He even uttered the hard words of confession so that she might not be ashamed, accepting only her agreement to what He said. He did not heed the fact that the Jews had no dealings with Samaritans, nor that His disciples marveled that He talked with a woman (Jn. 4: 9, 27).

True indeed are the words of St. John Chrysostom on God's love that God seeks a cause for our salvation even a tear shed ... God takes such a tear -before being caught by the devil of vain glory- as a cause for your salvation ... Indeed no heart is more compassionate for us than God's heart which is even more compassionate than our own hearts! He said, "*All day long I have stretched out My hands to a disobedient and contrary people*" (Rom. 10: 21) (Isa. 65: 2)! Even to such a disobedient people who follows only its own thoughts God stretches out His hands seeking their salvation! This reminds us of the Parable of the Sower.

The Lord accepted the tears of the woman who was a sinner and said to her "*Your sins are forgiven*", and said to those present "*her sins, which are many, are forgiven, for she loved much*", thus explaining to them how she was better than the Pharisee.

Those tears shed before God blotted out all the sinful past of that woman.

For her contrition the Lord did not remind her of her past sins. How beautiful in fact are the words of the Lord that He will never remember those sins.

The Parable of the Sower:

God compared Himself to a sower who sowed all the land.

He put His seeds in the good ground at all its levels; that which yielded a thirtyfold, that which yielded a sixtyfold, and that which yielded a hundredfold, all alike. God seeks all people to grant them the work of His grace, giving each His word of salvation. But what about the strong ground and the ground surrounded by thorns? Even these were visited by His grace. However, "*He who has ears to hear, let him hear!*" (Mt. 13: 9).

God seeks the salvation of all people, and does not keep His life-giving word from anyone.

His seeds fell even by the wayside and by the ground which had no depth of earth. So if God has worked with all those, you should have hope that He will work with you also that you might give fruit. If you do not give fruit, He will dig around you and fertilize you (Lk. 13: 8).

Hearken what beautiful comforting words are said in the Gregorian Holy Mass, [You did not leave me lacking any of Your glorious works. You surrounded me with all medicines leading to life]

If God was not good, He would not let His seeds fall even amidst thorns.

If we were in the same situation, we would say to such a land: pluck the thorns out that my seed may fall on you! God does not do that ... It is true that thorns do smother the plants in types of ground, but still God is able to pluck out thorns from any ground. He Himself digs around it, for some people cannot pluck out the thorns from themselves, but cry out with the words of inspiration, saying to the Lord,

"Resotre me, and I will return, for You are the Lord my God"(Jer. 31: 18).

Say with the psalmist, *"Purge me with hyssop, and I shall be clean; wash me, and I shall be white than snow"*(Ps. 51: 7). It is You, O Lord, who wash me and purge me. I will say with the leper, *"Lord, if You are willing, You can make me clean"*. Let me hear, O Lord the same words you said to him, *"I am willing; be cleansed"*.

God reconciles us to Himself:

God wants to reconcile us, and to correct us, with all possible means.

For this goal, He sent the apostles, the prophets, and the divine inspiration ... But why did He send those? Saint Paul the apostle gives the answer, *"God, who has reconciled us to Himself through Jesus Christ, and has given us the ministry of reconciliation ... Now then, we are ambassadors for Christ, as though God were pleading through us: we implore you on Christ's behalf, be reconciled to God"*(2 Cor. 5: 18, 20).

God, the kind-hearted, reconciled us to Himself not imputing to us our trespasses.

St. Paul says also, *"God was in Christ reconciling the world to Himself, not imputing their trespasses to them"* (2 Cor. 5: 19). And we conclude each of the Hours Prayers with the words [Our Christ, our good Lord ... calling all men to salvation for the promised forthcoming rewards].

God, in reconciling us and forgiving us, considers the weakness of our nature.

The Psalmist says, *"As far as the east is from the west, so far has He removed our transgressions from us. As a father pities his children, so the Lord pities those who fear Him. For He knows our frame, He remembers that we are dust."* (Ps. 103: 12-14). God descends to this dust, and reconciles it to Himself taking into consideration our weak nature.

Believe me, God does this even with those who flee from His presence!

We remember how God sought Adam when he fled from His presence and hid behind the trees (Gen. 3: 8). We remember also the story of Jonah the prophet.

The Story of Jonah the prophet

Jonah fled from the presence of the Lord, and the Lord sought his salvation.

Though Jonah fled to Tarshish, not obeying the Lord's command to go to Nineveh, the Lord did not reject him, not even in the second time when he became exceedingly displeased because the people of Nineveh repented and God had mercy upon them! Rather, God sought Jonah to be reconciled with Him and be convinced of His justice which previously made Jonah angry, even unto death!! (Jon. 4: 3, 4). See also the exceeding kindness of God in spite of Jonah's anger against God's will, as revealed in the Book of Jonah, *"And the Lord prepared a plant and made it come up over Jonah, that it might be shade for his head to deliver him from his misery"* (Jon. 4: 6).

The Book of Jonah gives us a beautiful example of how God seeks the salvation of humans.

The people of Nineveh would have not thought of their own salvation, nor the mariners of the ship in which Jonah fled, nor Jonah would have felt his fault and sought his own salvation, had not God Himself sought that and saved all of them.

It is God who started and took the initiative, then they

responded to His divine work. The response was immediate on the part of the mariners and the people of Nineveh, and after some time and persuasion on the part of Jonah the prophet.

God attracted the people in the ship by an amazing plan

God's plan worked through the mighty tempest that attacked the ship so that it was about to be broken, and through the fear that overwhelmed the mariners and made each of them cry out to his god, then through God's work in the lots they cast, through the confession of Jonah, and lastly by the calmness of the sea after throwing Jonah therein. The divine plan succeeded, as "*the men feared the Lord exceedingly, and offered a sacrifice to the Lord and took vows*"(Jon. 1: 16).

The mariners tried first their human means, but they failed, for they "*threw the cargo that was in the ship into the sea, to lighten the load*", but "*the sea continued to grow more tempestuous against them*". The men even rowed hard to return to land, but they could not. But God interfered by His own way to save them from the tempest and to save their lives spiritually, and God's plan for their salvation did succeed.

God attracted also the people of Nineveh by the divine warning through Jonah

The people of Nineveh were not able to save themselves; for they were of the gentiles away from faith, and were furthermore ignorant "*who cannot discern between their right and their left*"(Jon. 4: 11). However, God's warning that the city would be overthrown yielded its fruit, for the people of the city became afraid, repented and fasted, and moreover, "*they returned from their evil way; and God relented ...* "

The last was Jonah, who was also saved by God in two steps.

In the first step God sought the salvation of Jonah from the result of his disobedience and fleeing through the danger that attacked him in the sea. But Jonah was indifferent and was fast asleep at the time when the heathen mariners were praying so that the captain said to him, "*What do you mean, sleeper? Arise, call on your God, perhaps your God will consider us, so that we may not perish*"(Jon. 1: 6). The second step was the completion of the divine plan when God prepared a great fish to swallow Jonah (Jon. 1: 17).

At this point Jonah got rid of his disobedience, but he still needed to get rid of the love of being honored.

God overcame this by the sun that beat on Jonah's head, so that he grew faint, and by the plant that shaded him then was damaged by the worm. Lastly God argued with Jonah and succeeded in saving him as He saved before the people on the ship.

All of those responded to God's work in them, and for them. This leads us to another point:

Fellowship with God:

God works for you, seeking your salvation, so you have to respond.

You have to work with Him and not resist the work of the Spirit as the Jews and their fathers had done (Acts 7: 51), nor do as the bride of the Song did refusing to open for her beloved, for after waiting long for him, he turned away and was gone, so the bride said, "*My heart leaped up when he spoke. I sought him, but he gave me no answer ... I called him, but he gave me no answer*"(Song 5: 6).

The people at the time of Moses were unable to save themselves from the servitude of Pharaoh, and God Himself sought their salvation and delivered them, as Moses said to them, "*The Lord will fight for you, and shall hold your peace"*(Ex. 14: 14). However, it was important that the people respond to God's work and follow Him, and that they go through the Red Sea which God divided for them.

Be careful not to do as Agrippa, Felix, and the rich youth did.

King Agrippa received the call of salvation from God, was visited by grace and was affected, as he said to Paul the Apostle, *"You almost persuade me to become a Christian"*(Acts 26: 28). However, he did not take a positive step, but went away without being converted to Christianity.

Felix the governer also was visited by grace when st. Paul was speaking about righteousness, self-control, and the judgment to come. Felix was afraid, but he said to Paul, *"Go away for now; when I have a convenient time I will call for you"*(Acts 24: 25). He did not work with the Holy Spirit, and missed the opportunity given him.

Likewise, the young rich man had the chance of hearing the word of salvation from the mouth of Christ Himself, but he was subject to the lust of money, so, *"he went away sorrowful, for he had great possessions"*(Mt. 19: 22).

Know then that God seeks your salvation, and works for you, but you have to respond, to work with Him, or to submit to His work. See what true words st. Augustine says:

[God who created you without you, would not save you without you]

It means that God creates one without one's interference or participation, but with regard to salvation, it depends on one's response. Therefore you should work with Him. The Holy Spirit works within you, and you respond to the work of the Holy Spirit. So, *"Do not quench the Spirit"*(1 Thess. 5: 19); *"Do not grieve the Holy Spirit of God"*(Eph. 4: 30); Do not resist the Holy Spirit (Acts 7: 51). On the other hand, do have communion with the Spirit by working with Him, because God does not want to force you to love Him. Know that God's forbearance, longsuffering and goodness lead you to repentance (Rom. 2: 4). Do not lean on His forbearance, long suffering, love, and care and fall in indifference and carelessness; for the Holy Bible says, "*Today, if you will hear His voice, do not harden your hearts*"(Heb. 3: 15).

Various means and various ways:

God has many ways for leading people to Salvation

Some are called by God, others are left for some time till their hearts are inflamed with love and longing for Him, others still are attracted through temptations and tribulations, as He led Jonah to obedience by making the fish swallow him, and the people on the ship by the tempest, then by calming the tempest. Other people are attracted by mere warning as the people of Nineveh.

Do you complain then from temptations and tribulations? Perhaps God will save you through them!

Perhaps this is the only way fit for your character, or perhaps this way leads you to God sooner than other ways. So, when you face temptations, do not be annoyed, for they might be for your benefit.

Take the good of the temptation, and do not concentrate on the suffering of it.

God does not like to be hard to you, but if such hardness - within your power of endurance- is spiritually beneficial to you, it will be good temporarily.

The same applies to the period of suffering -which God determines according to one's benefit. As some food needs only a quarter of an hour on fire to be cooked, and other food needs two hours or more, so also one's nature determines the time length of suffering needed.

But, do not lose hope due to long time, it is for your good.

If you were weak and cannot bear the suffering, God is capable of helping you.

It is true that God seeks our salvation, but this does not mean that we take a passive attitude altogether, for grace does not assist the lazy. We have the words of the Lord, "*How often I wanted ... but you were not willing!*"(Mt. 23: 37). Say to Him then, "*Restore me, and I will return*"; "*Restore to me the joy of Your salvation*"; "*Bring back our captivity*". Submit your will to Him, and be sure that He will work within you, strengthening you. He will lead you in triumph, in the way that suits your nature, for God has many ways ...

If your power is limited, be faithful in what is least.

God was pleased with the person who had the two talents, and gave him the same blessing He gave to the one with the five talents (Mt. 25: 23, 21). God said to him the same words He said to the one with the five talents, "*Enter into the joy of your Lord*".

God does not request more than what is in your power, as what your weak nature can bear. Only be faithful in the little which you have.

Even if you do not have the little spiritually, God is able to give you. And if you are not able to be faithful in what is least, pray Him to give you the power and the faithfulness.

God who breathed on the dust and it became a living being, is able to breath into you so that you became a living spirit in His kingdom ...

CHAPTER 5

LITTLE THINGS

"Take heed that you do not despise one of these little

(Mt. 18: 10)

Some people aspire to have the lives of saints and the ranks they attained in the life of the spirit, or to deep attachment to God.

This may lead to mean-spiritedness, so one inquires: Am I, in this weak level, acceptable to God, though I have attained nothing that the saints have attained?

Would God accept this simple, little, trivial life of mine which is nothing compared to that of the saints?

Here I prefer to talk to you about God, the God of the lowly, who cares for the very little things and gives them a very high value. To our comfort, we are taught that:

"He raises the poor out of the dust, and lifts the needy out of the ash heap, that He may seat him with princes of His people"(Ps. 113: 7, 8)

God chose lowly individuals looked down at as worthless, but God knew their worth, or rather made them worthy. His hand stretched and raised them up.

1. God chose the young (the little in age):

David was young in the sight of his brothers, so he said about himself, *"I was small among my brothers, and the youngest in my father's house"* (Ps. 151: 1). But what did God do?

God took young David from among the sheep and made him the anointed of the Lord.

When Samuel the prophet went to anoint a king from

among the sons of Jesse the Bethlehemite, Jesse made his seven elder sons, who were of good appearance and physical stature, pass before Samuel: Eliab, Abinadab and the other five. But the Lord refused them. The Lord said about Eliab "*I have refused him*", and about each of the others, the prophet said, "*The Lord has not chosen these*" (1 Sam.16: 5-10). Finally, Jesse said:

"*There remains yet the youngest, and there he is, keeping the sheep*"(1 Sam. 16: 11)

Indeed, that youngest son whose father despised and left with the sheep, not allowed to be present at the celebration honored by the great prophet Samuel, that son was chosen by the Lord to be anointed.

The Spirit of the Lord came upon David from that day forward. And David became the man of the harp, the flute, and the instruments of ten strings, the most famous of the Old Testament prophets. Truly God does not look to the age, nor to outer appearance, and many times He did choose the young.

As God chose young David, He also chose Joseph the righteous, the youngest of his brothers.

God made Joseph king over all of them and over others as well. His brothers came to him, and fell before him on the ground though he was the youngest! God even made Joseph a father to Pharaoh and lord of all his house, and a ruler throughout all the land of Egypt (Gen. 45: 8).

God chose also Jeremiah the young prophet, who said, "*Behold, I cannot speak, for I am a youth*"(Jer. 1: 6).

The Lord said to young Jeremiah, "*Before I formed you in the womb I knew you; Before you were born I sanctified you; I ordained you a prophet to the nations ... Behold, I have put My words in your mouth. See, I have this day set you over the nations and over the kingdoms ... For behold, I have made you this day a fortified city and an iron pillar, and bronze walls against the whole land, against the kings of Judah, against its princes, against its priests, and against the people of the land"* (Jer. 1: 4, 5, 9, 10, 18).

We notice also that the most beloved disciple to the Lord Christ was the youngest: John.

The Lord considered John one of the three pillars (Gal. 2: 9), kept him alive longer than the others, gave him revelation of heaven, and made him writer of the most theological version of the gospel.

Among the young whom the Lord honored was **st. Mark the apostle**, who wrote the first gospel. Mark was a youth during the Lord Christ's life on earth, and started his ministry with st. Paul and st. Peter.

And st. Paul the apostle chose a youth to be a minister with him: Timothy, who became Bishop of Ephesus, to whom st. Paul said, *"Let no one despise your youth"* (1 Tim. 4: 12).

The great saint Amba Bishoy was also among the young chosen by the Lord.

The angel chose him to be a Nazirite to the Lord, though the slimmest, weakest, and youngest among his brothers. His mother suggested to the angel to choose one of his elder strong brothers to serve the Lord, but it was that slim, weak, young Bishoy that the Lord chose to be "The perfect man, beloved of the Lord Christ, who wash the feet of our Good Savior". Do not say then: I am young, for amazing is the Lord's choice of the young.

St. Athanasius the apostolic was still a youth during the Council of Nicaea.

In that ecumenical council, formed of 318 of the most famous bishops of the Christian world, Athanasius was yet a young deacon. However, God raised him to the top, and gave him power and victory over Arius to refute Arius' heresy and formulate the Christian Creed. This young deacon became the greatest theologian in the church history.

In the history of monasticism, among the greatest and most famous saints are Theodoros the disciple of st. Bachumius, st. John the short, and st. Misael the hermit.

God willed that the youth Theodoros be the spiritual guide in all st. Bachumius' monasteries. He even was the founder of those monasteries, and he appointed monks in charge of them ...

The young st. John the short was chosen by the Lord to be the spiritual guide in all Sheheit wilderness. The scetis was hung on his finger as monks used to say, and the monks usually gathered around him benefitting from his teaching. Though a young man, he had grace more than the elders!

There is also st. Misael who became a hermit at the age of 17.

It is worth noting also that the first monastery in Sheheit wilderness: Deir El Baramous, was called after the names of two young saints: Maximius and Domadius.

When God so willed that Goliath be conquered, He made a young man conquer him.

That young man, David, did not even know how to put on the war clothes being not used to them(1 Sam. 17: 38, 39). Instead, he used five smooth stones from the brook, and by those stones he killed Goliath and deserved to be anointed king by the Lord. So truly he sang, "*I was small among my brothers, and the youngest in my father's house ... My brothers were handsome and tall, but the Lord was not pleased with them*" (Ps. 151: 1, 5).

"*Take heed that you do not despise one of these little ones*" (Mt. 18: 10).

The Lord's care for children is very obvious in the Holy Bible. He set a little child in the midst of His disciples and said, "*unless you are converted and become as little children, you will by no means enter the kingdom of heaven*" (Mt. 18: 2, 3). The Lord said also, "*I thank You, Father ... that You have hidden these things from the wise and prudent and have revealed them to babes*" (Mt. 11: 25), and, "*But whoever causes one of these little ones who believe in Me to sin, it would be better for him if a millstone were hung around his neck, and he were drowned in the depth of the sea*" (Mt. 18: 6). Be then always aware that "*the battle is the Lord's*" (1 Sam. 17: 47), and "*nothing restrains the Lord from saving by many or by few*" (1 Sam. 14: 6).

Great indeed are the spiritual, intellectual, and technical gifts which God endowed the young with.

Many are the talents He gave the children and youth. David the prophet, for example, was talented in poetry and music, he became the man of the harp, the flue, and the instruments of the ten strings while still young. He was a clever player of the harp, and by it he could often make the distressing spirit depart from king Saul (1 Sam. 16: 23). Moreover, he was a valiant warrior in his youth.

St. Shenouti the Archimandrite, i.e. the head of anchorites, was spiritually gifted while still a boy.

St. Shenouti started fasting, prayers, and asceticism while yet a boy. In this, st. Mark the hermit resembled him, as the latter used also to fast to the nineth hour (i.e. three O'clock) though a child. It is a divine gift that shows God's care for children.

There is also st. Tekla Himanote who was endowed by God with the gift of working miracles while still a child.

These are not inherited capabilities, but divine gifts, which are not confined to the grown up, but the young also do enjoy them. Many are the saints who started their spiritual lives early because the grace of God so willed to work in them so early as has happened with Jeremiah who said he could not speak because he was a boy, and with Samuel the child, and also with Solomon who was only a youth.

The same spiritual maturity was endowed the holy Virgin while still young.

While a little orphan child, brought up in the Temple, she practiced deep prayers, contemplation, and study of Scriptures. Her famous praise song (Lk.1: 46-55) demonstrates how she memorized the psalms and verses while still young. It is the grace of God that worked in this Virgin full of grace, who was chosen in her childhood, and filled with God's gifts.

St. John Baptist was probably one of the gifted children.

This is clear in the words of the angel who announced his birth, "*He will also be filled with the Holy Spirit, even from his mother's womb*" (Lk. 1: 15), and the Holy Spirit worked in him while still in the womb. That is why he leaped in his mother's womb for joy when the greeting of the holy Virgin sounded in the ears of his mother (Lk. 1: 41-44).

The early maturity of the talented children has no explanation but that God's rich gifts are poured on children abundantly unspeakably.

Such gifts given children by God give us hope, so we repeat the words of the Lord of glory, "*I thank You, Father, ... that You have hidden these things from the wise and prudent and have revealed them to babes ... for so it seemed good in Your sight*" (Mt. 11: 25, 26).

What can we say about the early maturity of Athanasius, and his amazing childhood?

Nothing can be said except that God's gift is given abundantly and amazingly to children. The human mind stands confused before that and try to give it various causes, but the mind can find rest if the whole matter is ascribed to "God's gifts" and "God's love of children".

St. Athansius, who was called the apostolic, was the youngest that even sat on the see of st. Mark, and the greatest as well. He was a great hero of faith while yet young, and became patriarch in the age of thirty. In his youth he wrote great books such as "The Incarnation of the Word" and "A Letter to the Heathen".

We feel happy and are filled with hope when we know that the early maturity of children is due to God's gift and God's love.

It fills us with hope that God who gave those children His gifts abundantly, can also give us, provided that we feel humble and be like children according to His command, and furthermore, that we stand before Him empty.

Having talked about the little in age, we now talk about the little number:

2. God chose the young (the little in age):

God chose the little in number to give a blessing or work a miracle.

He chose the five loaves and two fish to work a great miracle

The Lord did not despise such a little amount, but blessed it, and with it He fed five thousand men. That little amount was also with a small lad (Jn. 6: 9). In the miracle of filling the four thousand of seven loaves and "*a few small fish*" (Mk. 8: 7), the amount was so small, and thousands of people were filled.

God chose such a little amount to give hope to every little thing.

God blesses the little and it becomes plenty; for it is not the number that avails, but the blessing which makes wonders.

So also in your ministry, do not lose hope because of your little talents, but say: Use me, O Lord, to feed Your people as if I were a few small fish.

In the Parable of the Sower, see what the Lord says about sowing in good ground:

"*... yielded a crop, some a hundredfold, some sixty, some thirty*" **(Mt. 13: 8)**

We understand, O Lord, that the ground (soil) that gives a hundredfold is a good soil, but how the one that gives a sixty or thirtyfold be called good? Is such a little crop acceptable to God?

But God says: So long as the ground has given fruit, it is good, even though the fruit is only thirty!

Let not then those with the thirty lose hope or fall in despair; for God accepts such little amount which is in their power and blesses it as if it were plenty. We say in the Oblations prayer:

[Those in abundance and those in scarcity ... Those who desire to offer to you but have none].

Even the intent to give, without actual giving, is acceptable to God who does not despise the little. Amazing indeed is God in His judgments and in His acceptance of the little! This reminds us of the words of one of the saints:

A blessing is in a cluster, even if it bears only one fruit.

The same meaning is repeated in (Isaiah 65: 8).

God works in the little so that we may not boast in our power thinking that we win by the plenty not by God's power, so we fall by such a thought.

This is clear in the story of the battle fought by Gideon with a small number.

Gideon had gathered a large army of thirty two thousand to fight the Midianites, but the Lord said to him, "*The people who are with you are too many for Me to give the Midianites into their hands, lest Israel claim glory for itself against Me, saying, 'My own hand has saved me'.* " (Jud. 7: 2). Then the Lord began to reduce that number until it became three hundred only, and blessed that small number, so they conquered the Midianites who were spread all over the valley as locusts.

In the New Testament, we read how the Lord chose twelve disciples only to preach the gospel.

In spite of so little a number, those disciples could preach the gospel to every creature (Mk. 16: 15), and to the end of the world their words have gone. Do not say then that you are a little number, for God blesses the little and it becomes a plenty. God restored the whole creation anew from only eight persons in the Ark.

From one son, Isaac, God brought forth descendants as plenty as the stars of heaven and the sand of the sea.

Now, having talked about God's care for the little in age, and the little in number, and how He blessed them, let's move to another point.

3. Care for the little in degree:

When God so willed that Goliath be defeated, He did so by a smooth stone from the sling of the small lad David.

Therefore, do not lose hope or think your talents are small. Do not say: I am young, of little importance, and not so strong as those who hate me. Be rather a small stone in the Lord's sling, and He will do good work with you whatever little power you have.

The battle is the Lord's (1 Sam. 17: 47); and nothing restrains Him from saving by many or by few (1 Sam. 14: 6).

Notice how He did spread His kingdom on the earth. He did not choose a group of philosophers, scholars, or valiant people, but He chose some simple fishermen and worked in them and through them, as the apostle says:

"God has chosen the foolish things of the world to put to shame the wise, and God has chosen the weak things of the world to put to shame the things which are mighty; and the base thing of the world and the things which are despised God has chosen, and the things which are not, to bring to nothing the things that are, that no flesh should glory in His presence" (1 Cor. 1: 27-29).

We stand speechless before these words! We can understand the wisdom behind choosing the foolish and the weak, but what about the despised and who are not? How can God choose those?! What an amazing thing!

Certainly these words revive hope within everyone, even though one is weak, not talented, with no capabilities or power whatsoever. Therefore, whenever you are fought with despair say: Account me, O Lord, among the despised and who are not, but do not deprive me from working with You. Let me have existence in Your sight, although -in my own sight and in the people's sight- I am despised and have no existence.

Some may perhaps think that if the Lord Christ came in our days, He would choose those with high academic degrees and professors.

Nay for sure! For He does not like flesh to glory in His presence, and lest the gospel should be ascribed to a human mind not to the Holy Spirit. If the Lord Christ did come in our days, it would not be strange if He chose some simple people or workers as he had done before.

The source of power is not man himself, but the Spirit of God who works in him.

That is why God likes to work with the young and the little so that they may not boast or lose hope in God's work with them. Therefore, let no one fail or be mean-spirited.

God spread the gospel through men who were not gifted.

Most of those evangelists were fishermen, but God worked in them. Even the thirteenth, St. Paul, did not depend on his education or gifts, as he said to the Corinthians, "*I, brethren, when I came to you, did not come with excellence of speech or of wisdom*" (1 Cor. 2: 1). The reason as he explained is "*not with wisdom of words, lest the cross of Christ should be made of no effect*" (1 Cor. 1: 17). In other words, lest Christianity be considered a kind of philosophy, or the success of preaching be ascribed to human wisdom not to the work of grace.

The gate of the kingdom is open to all, so is the gate of ministry

The gate of ministry is open to all, not only to those who say they have attained fullness and speak with tongues, not only those who have gifts and shake when praying, but also to the beginners and the novice in the field of ministry, those who cannot speak, for they are youth (Jer. 1: 6).

No one should think that unless he attains the top in spiritualities, he has not attained God!

And do not despise such persons who have not attained the top. Let not those feel mean-spirited, for God works in all and uses even "the few small fish". Hear the beautiful comforting words said by st. John Baptist:

"God is able to raise up children to Abraham from these stones" (Lk. 3: 8)

What do stones symbolize? They symbolize the deaf and dumb, i.e. those who cannot speak or move, in other words who has no life in them. Even of those, God is able to make children to Abraham. Do not, then, lose hope even though you have no life within you, for undoubtedly you are better than many stones.

Another clear example of God's care for the little is implied in the birth of the Lord Christ:

The Lord Christ was born in a manger, not in a big palace; and in a small village, Bethlehem, not in the great city Jerusalem.

However, he could turn the manger into an ecumenical place visited by the whole world, and one most holy. And to Bethlehem He said, "*you, Bethlehem ... are not the least among the rulers of Judah*" (Mt. 2: 6). He raised it above countries and gave it honor by being born in it.

This reminds us of God's call to Gideon who felt mean-spirited because of his base origin and small country, he said to God, "*Indeed my clan is the weakest in Manasseh, and I am the least in my father's house*" (Jud. 6: 15). But God was searching for such a person to reveal His glory in him.

Do not, therefore, lose hope for being young, for being a manger or a small village, for being the least in your father's house, or because your clan is the weakest! God is able to work in you, and to raise you to become completely different to an extent you have never thought of.

Such examples give courage to the weak and humble, and to the little and despised.

An amazing case is the choice of Moses the prophet. Moses was not eloquent, but slow of speech and slow of tongue (Ex. 4: 10), **but God chose him to be God's spokesman!** God did not remove this defect from Moses, but sent his brother Aaron with him to be as a mouth for him. Then God said to Moses, "*I will be with your mouth and teach you what you shall say*" (Ex. 4: 12, 15).

Lack of talents does not restrain God's work, and does not mean that one loses hope in carrying out one's responsibilities. But one should put all confidence in God who said about Himself, "*He gives power to the weak, and to those who have no might He increases strength*" (Isa. 40: 29).

God also uses the little things for a certain purpose. Let us see, when God led Jonah the prophet to repentance and reconciliation, how did He do that?

To restore Jonah, God used the worm, the plant, the wind, the tempest, and the sun. Each of these things performed a divine message (Jon. 1, 4)

The plant which came up in a night and perished in a night, was used by God to realize His intents, and also the worthless worm. So say to God: Account me, O Lord, as a worm, a plant, a wind, or a sun ray. Let me be anything -however worthless- in Your kingdom, but let me do Your will.

And if you are a worm, lose not hope; for you will have your role with God. If you are a plant, be not mean-spirited; for time will come when you give a lesson to a prophet like Jonah, and have your name mentioned in the Book of Life!

4. God's care for the little things:

* **The Lord cared for children, and spoke of them with all love and consideration.**

The Lord took the children in His bosom in love and said, *"Let the little children come to Me, and do not forbid them; for of such is the kingdom of heaven"* (Mt. 19: 14). Then the Lord called a little child and set him in the midst, and said to His disciples, *"Unless you are converted and become as little children, you will by no means enter the kingdom of heaven. Therefore whoever humbles himself as this little child is the greatest in the kingdom of heaven. Whoever receives one little child like this in My name receives Me."* (Mt. 18: 2-5).

* **The Lord cared for the souls of the little and warned against causing them to stumble.**

He said, *"whoever causes one of these little ones who believe in Me to sin, it would be better for him if a millston were hung around his neck, and he were drowned in the depth of the sea"* (Mt. 18: 6).

God cares for the little, whether the little in age, in spirituality, or in weakness. His care encompasses all.

* **He cared even for the bruised reed and the smoking flax.**

The Bible says about the Lord, *"A bruised reed he will not break, and smoking flax He will not quench"* (Mt. 12: 20). He gave hope to both; the bruised reed may be tied together, and the smoking flax may burn again by some wind He sends.

* **He gave hope and a new chance to the tree that gave no fruit.**

When the ax was laid to the root of the tree to cut it down, He said in kindness, *"let it alone this year also, until I dig around it and fertilize it. And if it bears fruit, well. But if not, after that you can cut it down"* (Lk. 13: 7-9). He did not lose hope even in that tree which gave no fruit for three years.

* He gives importance even to the little ant, and present it as a lesson to people.

He says, *"Go to the ant, you sluggard! Consider her ways and be wise"* (Prov. 6: 6). But we inquire: What is the ant, O Lord, that You save her and give her such an active nature, giving her as an example of activity, skill, and power given her by You, And God, as if answering, says:

Think not that I am the creator of the dragons and beasts, but I created also the insects and I do care for those and these. I care even for the birds of which two are sold for one coin, and give food to the young ravens that cry to Me (Ps. 147: 9). Amazing indeed that God creates these little things and cares for them. Even the worm creeping under the stone, or the lilies which Solomon in all his glory was not arrayed like one of them (Mt. 6: 29), they enjoy God's care.

* The Lord gives us the mustard seed which is the least of all the seeds as an example of faith and the kingdom of heaven.

He says, *"The kingdom of heaven is like a mustard seed, which a man took and sowed in his field, which indeed is the least of all the seeds; but when it is grown it is greater than the herbs and becomes a tree, so that the birds of the air come and nest in its branches"* (Mt. 13: 31-32).

The Lord says also, *"If you have faith as a mustard seed, you will say to this mountain, 'Move from here to there', and it will move; and nothing will be impossible for you"* (Mt. 17: 20).

So, do not lose hope even though your faith is so small as a mustard see; for it may grow and become a tree and birds nest in it. God does accept this faith and bless it.

* **The little leaven that leavens the whole lump is another example given by the Lord for faith and the kingdom of heaven.**

The Lord says, "*The kingdom of heaven is like leaven, which a woman took and hid in three measures of meal till it was all leavened*" (Mt. 13: 33). St. Paul remembered this parable and said to the Galatians, "*A little leaven leavens the whole lump*" (Gal. 5: 9). Do not lose hope then however little was your faith, and however small was your effort; for God accepts the little and blesses it to become much.

* **The lord gave hope even to the maimed and the lame.**

He said to the servant who prepared the great supper, "*Go out into the streets and lanes of the city, and bring in here the poor and the maimed and the lame and the blind*" (Lk. 14: 21). He commanded also that when one gives a feast, one should invite the poor, the maimed, the lame, the blind. One will be blessed for this because they cannot repay (Lk. 14: 13). So if you are fought with losing hope, remember those who have nothing to repay and God accepted them though having nothing.

* **In the miracle of the five loaves and the two fish we notice that God cared for the fragments and ordered His disciples to gather them up.**

You may probably say: Would I be a loaf in the Lord's hand, that He may bless me and feed thousands of me, that I be able to correct something in the ministry! But, even if you were not a loaf but just a fragment on the floor which no one would eat, you will hear the Lord's word "*gather up the fragments*". Time will come and you will be able to fill others.

So, if your spiritual activity is weak, say to the Lord humbly: Accept me, O Lord, in Your kingdom among the poor, the maimed, the lame, and the blind. And as You cared for the fragment in the miracle, account me also one of these fragments that I may be carried by Your apostles in their baskets. Add me to Your blessed basket.

Think not that you have to go up to meet God, but so long as you feel worthless and so long as you consider yourself nothing and your heart is humbled, then you will meet God. As you go downward, so also you will go up.

Truly one goes up when he goes down, and goes down when he goes up, as the Lord says, *"For whoever exalts himself will be humbled, and he who humbles himself will be exalted"* (Lk. 14: 11)

* **In His care for the little, the Lord accepts the repentants and search for them as in the three parables He gave in (Lk. 15)**

The Lord gave us the parable of **the Prodigal Son** who returned with contrite heart and was accepted with great joy and many rewards. There is also the parable of **the Lost Sheep**. Who has a hundred sheep and notices that there is one lost, and goes after it till he finds it and returns rejoicing with it on his shoulders? Or who ever cares for **one lost coin** and searches for it carefully and rejoices when it is found? Does not this give you hope that God works for you? He searches for you even if you do not seek Him!

* **In His care for the little, God cared for the small village of Bethlehem**

The divine inspiration said about Bethlehem, *"you ... are not the least among the rulers of Judah"*; for He chose it to be a holy place for the glorious nativity of the Lord.

* **In His care for the little, God chose Leah who was unloved and whose eyes were delicate (Gen. 29: 17)**

Leah was unloved and Jacob preferred Rachel to her, but God chose Leah to be the mother of Judah the origin of kings, and Levi the origin of priesthood, and to be the grandmother of the Lord Christ who came from her offspring not the offspring of her sister Rachel.

* God chose also Rahab the harlot, Tamar, and Ruth the Moabite among the Lord's genealogy (Mt. 1: 3, 5). He even chose Mary Magdalene, who had seven demons, to convey the joyful message to the apostles (Mk. 16: 9, 10). However, He chose dust to make of it His image and likeness! Do not lose hope then that God will work with you and choose you.

* *"He raises the poor out of the dust, and lifts the needy out of the ash heap, that He may seat him with the princes of His people"* **(Ps. 112: 7, 8)**

God is able to raise you from your low state, and lift you even to sit with the princes of your people. Isn't it He who does not despise a bruised reed and a smoking flax, and commands us to comfort the fainthearted, to uphold the weak, and to be patient with all (1 Thess. 5: 15). What beautiful words He says, *"strengthen the hands which hang down, and the feeble knees"* (Heb. 12: 12). Be sure then that even if you are of this kind, God will not forsake you, but will send you who will raise you.

* **Take for example His care for the sparrows to be sure of His care for you.**

He says, *"Are not two sparrows sold for a copper coin? And not one of them falls to the ground apart from your Father's will."* (Mt. 10: 29). This is an example of His care for everyone; for He says immediately following that, *"But the very hairs of your head are all numbered. Do not fear therefore; you are of more value than many sparrows"* (Mt. 10: 30). The Lord admires the birds because they trust that God feeds them so they do not bother about searching for food. He says, *"Look at the birds of the air, for they neither sow nor reap nor gather into barns; yet your heavenly Father feeds them"* (Mt. 6: 26). The Lord mentions these and the young ravens that cry (Ps. 147: 9) as an example for us.

* **He cares even for the worm under the stone and gives it its food.**

The more so He cares for you and gives you the food of the spirit as well as the food of the body. Is not man better than many worms? The small worm was used by God as a lesson to Jonah the prophet when He made it damage the plant (Jn. 4: 7). It is merely a worm but it is mentioned in the Scriptures and had a message which led to the repentance of a prophet.

5. God cares for little actions:

God does not forget the cup of cold water offered to a thirsty person.

He says, "*Whoever gives one of these little ones only a cup of cold water in the name of a disciple, assuredly, I say to you, he shall by no means lose his reward*" (Mt. 10: 42; Mk. 9: 41).

Just a cup of cold water which you did not labor or pay for, its reward is not lost. So do not fall in despair because your works are little.

* **The small actions you do and forget for their being so small, are not forgotten by God.** Even if they are worthless in your sight, they have their value in god's sight, and you will be rewarded for them on the Last Day. However, it is better that you forget them so that you may be fully rewarded for them there, in eternity.

* **The Lord praised the queen of the South, merely because she visited Solomon.**

He said, "*The queen of the South will rise up in the judgment with this generation and condemn it, for she came from the ends of the earth to hear the wisdom of Solomon"* (Mt. 12: 42).

* **The Lord praised also the widow of Zarephath Sidon who hosted Elijah the prophet in the days of the famine (Lk. 4: 25, 26).**

* **He did not forget the visit of Nicodemus though he came to Him by night in fear.**

The Lord permitted that this visit be recorded in the gospel (Jn. 3). He blessed and developed this frightened hidden faith of Nicodemus and let him bound His body in linen with spices for burial. This Nicodemus became afterwards one of the most famous Christians and a good worker in the field of ministry.

* **The Lord did not forget Zacchaeus because he just climbed up the sycamore tree to see Him.**

Probably, Zacchaeus did not think that what he had done is a great work to be rewarded by the Lord. But the Lord, who cares for every small action, stood, called Zacchaeus, and went into his house and said to him, *"Today salvation has come to this house, because he also is a son of Abraham"* (Lk. 19: 9). Has it even occurred to Zacchaeus that the Lord will account his climbing up the sycamore tree so worthy?! But it is the Lord who cares for ever little work.

* **He did not forget the humble words uttered by the Canaanite woman.**

He praised her, saying, *"... great is your faith! Let it be to you as you desire."*, and He healed her daughter from that very hour (Mt. 15: 28).

* **He never forgot that His people went after Him in the wilderness though they were grumbling and hard-hearted.**

He said, *"I remember you ... when you went after Me in the wilderness, in a land not sown"* (Jer. 2: 2). Although the people made many faults in the wilderness, grumbled and were stiff-necked and ungrateful, but there mere coming out after the Lord to worship Him in the wilderness was not forgotten by Him.

And in the New Testament, He said to His disciples, "*But you are those who have continued with Me in My trials*" (Lk. 22: 28). This He said in spite of their weak steadiness. They even could not watch with Him one hour (Mt. 26: 40)! Some of them were afraid and fled when he was arrested, and Peter denied Him thrice. Only st. John was with Him at the cross, however, following Him and holding to Him as their Master, though considered as nothing by them, was never forgotten by the Lord.

* **In the same way, the Lord praised those who came at the eleventh hour.**

Though they began work at the end of the day and worked only one hour, he accepted this one hour work and gave them as the others. He did not refuse this little work, but rather praised it; for this at least shows that they are fruitful and able to work.

* **As He accepted this little from the workers, He accepted also the two mites from the widow.**

He praised her, saying that she had put in more than all because she -out of her poverty- put in all that she had (Mk. 12: 44). The two mites are very small and worthless, but giving out of one's poverty is very great in god's sight whatever quantity is given.

* **Likewise if you pray only for few minutes out of your needed time, God will accept these minutes ...**

If time is lacking, and you found none but some moments to raise your heart to God, do not be disheartened or lose hope for not praying as should be. Nay, God examines the hearts and knows your circumstances. He knows whether it is out of disregard and carelessness or given out of need.

* **The prayer of the tax-collector was very short, just one sentence, but God accepted it.**

The tax-collector went to his house justified than the Pharisee (Lk. 18: 9-14) because he was praying with all his heart and with contrition, not daring to lift his eyes upwards. Therefore, the one sentence he uttered was in God's sight very valuable and appreciated. God did not ask the tax-collector about high level spiritual practice as required from saints, but He was satisfied with the contrition of the tax-collector.

* **God accepted also the repentance of the thief on the right hand of the Lord at the last hours of his life (Lk. 23: 43). He was satisfied as well with the words of the Samaritan woman which He considered as confession though she did not explain everything (Jn. 4). Likewise, He praised the unjust steward-in spite of his faults- merely for his being careful about his own future (Lk. 16: 8)**

* **Do not then fall in despair if your spiritual work is weak and your fruit is little.**

Do not say: 'No use, I have done nothing', and fall in despair because of that. Know rather that God never forgets any simple work which you may have done and forgotten. He did not forget the Queen of the South who travelled to hear the wisdom of Solomon, and because of such little work -as it seems- He said that she would rise up in the judgement with that generation and condemn it (Mt. 12: 42).

St. John Chrysostom asserts God's care for the little, saying, [**God seeks some reason for your salvation, even one tear you shed**]

Indeed, God is satisfied with the little provided that it is with good spirit, and one is unable to do more. He takes this little, develops and multiplies it. Do not fall then in despair or let the devil fight you saying: What have you done while God wants you to be perfect (Mt. 5: 48)?

It is true that God requires you to be perfect, but He does not ask you to do more than you can.

He takes into consideration -when charging you- your capabilities and circumstances, and accepts gradual advancement. He wants you just to be on your way, not to have reached the end. He gives you the chance and waits with long-suffering to lead you to repentance.

However God's forbearance should not make us indifferent and lax!

Our little fruit does not mean that we remain satisfied with it! Nay, we should struggle and grow in hope and without falling in despair, but rather asking God to strengthen our weakness and give us His grace and help to do always what pleases Him ...

CHAPTER 6

God The Loving and Compassionate

Man is hard, but God is loving, kind, and compassionate; therefore when David was given the option to choose one of three punishments, he said his famous word "*Let us fall into the hand of the Lord, for His mercies are great; but do not let me fall into the hand of man*" (2 Sam. 24: 14). And when Job the righteous fell in the hands of his three friends, they did not stop blaming and accusing him, so he said to them, "*How long will you torment my soul, and break me in pieces with words? These ten times you have reproached me*" (Job 19: 2, 3). Unlike man, God is merciful and compassionate as we shall see from the following examples:

God's commandments are within our power:

God started with us gradually from the Old Testament commandments to the perfection of the New Testament. He blamed the scribes and Pharisees for laying on men's shoulders heavy burdens hard to bear which they themselves could not move with one of their fingers. He explained to them that by this they shut up the kingdom of heaven against men, and they neither went in nor allowed those who were entering to go in (Mt. 23: 4, 13).

In the same way, in the first council held in Jerusalem to discuss the acceptance of the Gentiles into faith, the Lord's disciples said, "*we should not trouble those from among the Gentiles who are turning to God, but that we write to them to abstain from things polluted by idols, from sexual immorality, from things strangled, and from blood*" (Acts 15: 19, 20). And St. Paul the apostle said to the Corinthians, "*I fed you with milk and not with solid food; for until now you were not able to receive it*" (1 Cor. 3: 2).

God is so loving and compassionate that He gives with the commandment the power to carry it out. His grace accompanies us so that we may be able to comply with the commandment, and He gives us His Holy Spirit to work within us to be able to act.

In His compassion, God's loving care extends to all the creation, even to animals and nature, not only to man.

God's love and compassion for animals:

God gave the Sabbath for rest to man, and to animals as well. He said, "*the seventh day is the Sabbath of the Lord your God. In it you shall do no work: you, nor your son, nor your daughter, nor your male servant, nor your female servant, nor your ox, nor your donkey, nor any of your cattle*" (Deut. 5: 14).

God did not only care for the rest of the animals, but He also cared for the rest of the land.

He said, "*Six years you shall sow your land and gather in its produce, but the seventh year you shall let it rest and lie fallow*" (Ex. 23: 10, 11; Lev. 25: 3-5). However, in spite of this stress on keeping the Sabbath and not working in it, the Lord said, "*Which of you, having a donkey or an ox that has fallen into a pit, will not immediately pull him out on the Sabbath day?*" (Lk. 14: 5), "*What man is there among you who has one sheep, and if it falls into a pit on the Sabbath, will not lay hold of it and lift it out*" (Mt. 12: 11), and He said also to the person who blamed Him for healing on the Sabbath the woman who was bent over because of a spirit of infirmity, "*Hypocrite! Does not each one of you on the Sabbath loose his ox or donkey from the stall, and lead it away to water it? So ought not this woman, being a daughter of*

Abraham ... be loosed from this bond on the Sabbath?" (Lk. 13: 15).

By this example the Lord made the saving or feeding of an ox, a donkey, or a sheep an obligatory exception from the commandment of not working on the Sabbath day.

His mercy on animals is apparent also in the command, *"You shall not boil a young goat in its mother's milk"*, and, *"You shall not muzzle an ox while it treads out the grain"* (1 Cor. 9: 9). That is why up till now no ox is muzzled while threshing, but is left to eat whatever it likes.

Another example of God's care for animals is His words, *"You shall not plow with an ox and a donkey together"* (Deut. 22: 10).

The reason is that their power is not equal, so if the ox hastens, the donkey will get tired, and God does not like this. That is why the Lord Christ entered Jerusalem sitting on a donkey and a colt, the foal of a donkey (Mt. 21: 5) in order to move from one to the other and let the first take some rest. God's compassion towards animals is also clear in His reproach to Balaam for striking his donkey unjustly (Num. 22: 32).

His compassion extends also to the sparrows and birds, feeding and protecting them.

He says, *"Are not two sparrows sold for a copper coin? And not one of them falls to the ground apart from your Father's will"* (Mt. 10: 29) i.e. no sparrow will fall to the ground unless He permits that. He says also, *"Look at the birds of the air, for they neither sow nor reap nor gather into barns; yet your heavenly Father feeds them"* (Mt. 6: 26). The psalms also assert the same:

"He gives to the beast its food, and to the young ravens that cry" **(Ps. 147: 9).**

O Lord, even the young ravens!! Yes, they even were entrusted with some duty at the time of famine, they brought bread and meat to feed Elijah the prophet (1 Kgs. 17: 4-6). This happened with st. Paul the anchorite. As He was compassionate towards the birds, the sparrows, and the beasts, the Lord cared also for the lost sheep and searched for it until He found it (Lk. 15).

God cared for the animals and birds in our father Noah's ark!

He brought into the ark all animals, beasts, birds, and even every creeping thing, to let them live. Our father Noah gave them food every day. How amazing such wonderful caring!

God's care for animals appears in protecting them from nature and from being devoured by other fierce animals.

God has given the bear and the fox living in the pole regions thick shaggy fur to keep them warm in the very cold weather they live in, while the animals living in hot countries do not have such fur. The camel, for example, because it lives in the desert, is given by God great power to endure thirst and hunger. This same power is given by God to the palm trees that grow in the desert.

God provides fierce animals with paws and incisors to be able to survive, and at the same time provides weak animals with means of flight!

The lion is stronger than the gazelle and can devour it, but the gazelle is given by God swiftness and amazing power to run away from the lion. Likewise, the dog can kill the cat, but cats are given the power to jump over trees and walls to escape from dogs. The birds are also given the power of flying to be safe, and the rats the power of digging in earth and hiding safely ... what wonderful caring of God is all this!

Look what beautiful voice is given the singing nightingale and birds! Look what graceful shape is given the peacock and the butterfly! How fragrant are roses and jasmine and other beautiful scented flowers! Look what wonderful capabilities bees are endowed with to build their houses according to very accurate engineering, to make honey from nectar, and to make their queens' food, which people use as food and medicine! Look also how the ant is active and assiduous! God gives His creation such qualities as a model which man may aspire to acquire.

If such is God's care for His creation, how rather more would be His care for man!

God's great love and compassion for man:

Suffice that God created man with a distinguished nature: with intellect, spirit, and free will.

Man is endowed with intellect and so was able to invent, to make satellites and space ships, to reach the moon, and to walk on the space where there is no gravity. God gave man free will by which one can do whatever he likes, and gave intelligence to all people, even to the wicked who disobey Him! And beyond these natural gifts, God gave some people super natural gifts such as the power to work miracles. How wonderful is it that man is created in God's image, after His likeness (Gen. 1).

God granted man immortality and eternal life.

Man is given an eternal life in God's kingdom after the resurrection of the body, and is promised eternal happiness in communion with God's angels in the heavenly Jerusalem "*the tabernacle of God .. with men*" (Rev. 21: 3). He even said to the righteous, "*where I am, there you may be also*" (Jn. 14: 3). He promised those who love Him to enjoy a wonderful life in eternity of which it is written, "*Eye has not seen, nor ear heard, nor have entered into the heart of man the things which God has prepared for those who love Him*" (1 Cor. 2: 9).

God's love made Him call men His children.

As st. John the apostle says, "*Behold what manner of love the Father has bestowed on us, that we should be called children of God!*" (1 Jn. 3: 1). God so willed that we address Him "*Our Father in heaven*" (Mt. 6: 9), and He says to us, "*No longer do I call you servants ... but I have called you friends*" (Jn. 15: 15).

So our relationship with God is one of love.

It is written, "*Having loved His own who were in the world, He loved them to the end*" (Jn. 13: 1). He likened this love to the love of a father for his children, and as David the prophet said in the psalm, "*As a father pities his children, so the Lord pities those who fear Him*" (Ps. 103: 13). His love is so great that He called us His bride and described this love symbolically in the Song of Songs.

The depth of God's love for man appears in the sacrifice and redemption He made.

"*For God so loved the world that He gave His only begotten Son, that whoever believes in Him should not perish but have everlasting life*" (Jn. 3: 16). And the Lord Christ said, "*You are My friends if you do whatever I command you*", "*Greater love has no one than this, than to lay down one's life for his friends*" (Jn. 15: 14, 13). Because of this love, and for sacrificing and redemption, He became incarnate and emptied Himself (Phil. 2: 7). This redemption was described by the prophet, "*All we like sheep have gone astray; we have turned, every one, to his own way; and the Lord has laid on Him the iniquity of us all*" (Isa. 53: 6).

Out of His love for us, God gave us repentance as a means for forgiveness of sins.

God did not insist on punishing us for our sins, but He opened for us a door for salvation through repentance. As written in the Holy Bible, "*God has also granted to the Gentiles repentance to life*" (Acts 11: 18); "*there will be more joy in heaven over one sinner who repents than over ninety-nine just persons who need no repentance*" (Lk. 15: 7); "*You have chastised me, and I was chastised*" (Jer. 31: 18); and, "*God who always leads us in triumph in Christ*" (2 Cor. 2: 14).

Due to His compassion towards man, God gave him the divine inspiration.

God "*at various times and in various ways spoke in time past to the fathers by the prophets*" (Heb. 1: 1). He gave humans His commandments and talked with Moses, and with Abraham as well. He gave us the written Law and the prophecy with which "*holy men of God spoke as they were moved by the Holy Spirit*" (2 Pet. 1: 21). Thus God taught us His ways, made us understand, and enlightened our eyes so as not to go astray.

God gave us His Holy Spirit to abide in us, and made us a dwelling place for His Holy Spirit.

As st. Paul the apostle says, "*Do you not know that you are the temple of God and that the Spirit of God dwells in you?*"(1 Cor. 3: 16). As the Spirit of God descended upon people and in them, He worked in them and they gave the fruit of the Spirit (Gal. 5: 22, 23). They began to have various gifts of the Spirit (1 Cor. 12), and began to have communion with the Holy Spirit (2

Cor. 13: 14) even to the extent that they became "*partakers of the divine nature*" (2 Pet. 1: 4), which means that they take part in working for salvation, not that they acquire the divine essence and nature.

Out of God's compassion, He gave man blessing and grace.

God's blessings are innumerable, and His grace is beyond imagining and needs a long talk. God's blessing began since the creation of man, and continued with the fathers and the righteous. He said to our father Abraham, "*I will bless you ... and you shall be a blessing*" (Gen. 12: 2), thus we hear about the blessings given the children by their fathers.

Protection, dispensation, and ministry of angels for men are a clear manifestation of God's compassion towards man.

What beautiful and comforting words are those said about angels, "*Are not all ministering spirits sent forth to minister for those who will inherit salvation?*" (Heb. 1: 14). There are innumerable examples of angels' interference for saving people or leading them to faith. Due to God's compassion, we will be "*like angels of God in heaven*" (Mt. 22: 30), and some people are even called angels, like the angels of the churches mentioned in (Rev. 2, 3) and like John Baptist (Mk. 1: 2). Moreover, many beautiful tales are told about the guarding angel.

In temptation, God -out of His compassion- is with us.

He does not allow us to be tempted beyond what we are able to endure, and with the temptation He gives the way of escape, so that we may be able to bear it. He even gives crowns and blessing, provided that we receive His love and compassion with love, and not with indifference.

CHAPTER 7

"*I am with you and will keep you wherever you go, and will bring you back to this land*

(Gen. 28: 15)

Let us contemplate on God's words to our father Jacob the Patriarch; God said to him,

"Behold, I am with you and will keep you wherever you go, and will bring you back to this land; for I will not leave you until I have done what I have spoken to you" (Gen. 28: 15)

1. Persons brought back to their land:

* **Jacob the Patriarch**: He came out of his father's house afraid of his brother Esau. He went on his way not knowing what was awaiting him, putting only before him his mother's advice, *"Surely your brother Esau comforts himself concerning you by intending to kill you. How therefore, my son, obey my voice: arise, flee to my brother Laban in Haran. And stay with him a few days, until your brother's anger turns away from you ..."* (Gen. 27: 43-45). And on his way, fleeing from his brother's anger and intention to kill him, God comforted him, saying, *"I am with you and will keep you wherever you go, and will bring you back to this land"*!

It is God's compassion and protection

Our good, kind-hearted God accompanies a person who is fleeing from injustice or persecution, keeping him wherever he goes and brings him back to his land !

God's compassion in this story appears in being offered to a weak, incapable person:
- Our father Jacob was unable to protect himself.
- He was much weaker than Esau who was capable of killing him.

- Jacob was incapable of keeping himself on the way or of coming back to his land.

Thus God, the God of the weak, interfered to keep, protect, and bring back.

In fact in everyone's life there is a divine work, accompanied by promises giving hope to the troubled soul. And the stories of the scriptures include many examples of such divine work:

* **God's people**: As God fulfilled His promise to one person: Jacob, He also fulfilled it to a whole people. They were taken captives to Babylon and Assyria, where they lived in servitude, unable to protect themselves. They were in distress and they hung their harps upon willows and sang the psalm, "*By the rivers of Babylon, there we sat down, yea, we wept when we remembered Zion*" (Ps. 137: 1). Here God interfered and whispered in the ears of the people a word of hope, "*Behold, I am with you and will keep you wherever you go, and will bring you back to this land*". And it so happened as Nehemia joyfully tells the story of their return and God's great work with them.

The people were freed from captivity, they returned and rebuilt the broken down walls of Jerusalem, and repaired its burnt gates. The Lord brought them back to their land!

* **Our father Adam, who was in a worse state**: when he sinned and broke the commandment, God drove him out of the garden of Eden and placed cherubim with a flaming sword which turned every way to guard the way to the tree of life lest Adam and Eve eat from it. God said that Adam in toil shall eat of the ground all the days of his life, and the gates of the garden (Paradise) were closed (Gen. 3). But what further?

Amidst all this trouble, and in spite of the punishment and dismissal, the same divine promise was made to our father Adam "*Behold, I am with you and will keep you wherever you *go, and will bring you back to this land*"! But when did God bring him back to Paradise? This happened five thousand years later! But it did happen.

God's promises are kept however long they continue unfulfilled.

Thousands of years passed, but the comforting words of God "*I am with you ... and will bring you back to this land*" has never vanished from the mind of any of the fathers.

They all rest in hope

Each of them say the words of the psalm, "*... I had believed that I would see the goodness of the Lord in the land of the living. Wait on the Lord ...*" (Ps. 27: 13, 14). God does not always strive with us, nor keeps His anger forever (Ps. 103: 9). He drove Adam out of the garden because he sinned, however, He gave him the promise of salvation ... And our Lord Jesus Christ was crucified bearing all our sins and paying the wages of sin in full to the divine justice. What did happen then?

The Lord opened the gates of Paradise and brought Adam back to that land!

The Lord restored also all Adam's children, who departed in hope, as well as the thief on the Lord's right hand who also departed with hope in the divine promise, "*Today, you will be with Me in Paradise*".

We also praise the Lord, saying to Him: True indeed are Your promises, O Lord, and real is every hope you provide.

Yes Lord, when You tell someone that You will bring him back to this land, You certainly do. You brought back Jacob the patriarch to his land after twenty years, the people in captivity to their homeland after seventy years, and our father Adam to Paradise after more than 5000 years.

God's promises are certainly fulfilled even though after

twenty, seventy, or five thousand years ...

But sure God will fulfill His promise, at the time He determines, with His love and power. He restores the souls He has promised, thus the power of the divine work shall be manifested in the lives of the individuals and congregation.

Two remarks are noted from the three preceding examples:

The three preceding examples deal with disabled, or rather, sinful persons.

Our father Jacob was unable to come back to his land, the people in captivity were also unable to return, and Adam as well was absolutely unable to return to Paradise. These are examples of souls that sinned against the Lord, and therefore were not worthy of His promises.

Adam's sin, or rather numerous sins*, are well known. And Jacob deceived his blind father and obtained the blessing through deceit, and the firstborn right from his brother by leaving him on the verge of death of hunger. The people of Israel had fallen in the worship of idols, besides many other sins that raised God's anger and made Him deliver them to the hands of their enemies.

However, God does not give His promises and protection only to the righteous, but even to sinners.

---

* See our book "Adam and Eve".

Even sinners do not fall from God's care and protection; for if they were deprived of God's care, no one would be saved. But the Lord came to seek and save that which is lost, and he declared that it is the sick who need the physician, not those who are well, and that He came to call sinners -not righteous- to repentance.

* **Many indeed are God's promises to sinners, to bring them back to the land.**

Even in man's fall, and in his sin, the Lord says to him, I am with you, and will bring you back to this land, the land of living. The lost sheep which went out of its pen and was lost, and did not know how to come back, heard the words of the Lord, "*I am with you and will keep you wherever you go, and will bring you back to this land*". Then the Lord carried it in His arms joyfully and brought it back to where it had been. Likewise, the lost coin could not have returned to the pocket or box of its owner had not the Lord been with it, kept it, and restored it to the land.

* **Another example is the story of Jonah the Prophet.**

In his sin, Jonah was cast into the sea and swallowed by the fish, and he remained there in the fish belly. Who could bring him out? But, while in the belly of the fish, he prayed to the Lord to let him return and see again His holy temple. And the Lord looked at him while in the belly of the fish and said, "*Behold, I am with you and will keep you ... and will bring you back to the land*", and it so happened.

How amazing God is! Everything is possible to Him, even what seems impossible to people.

* Had it ever occurred to the three young men while being cast into the furnace of fire that they would come back home? But amidst the fire, the Lord whispered in the ears of each of them, "*I am with you ... and will bring you back to the land*"

* Daniel as well, while in the lion's den in the middle of the hungry lions, heard the same words of the Lord. And God did bring Daniel safe out of the den, as He brought out the three young men from the furnace and Jonah from the belly of the fish.

Wonderful indeed is the Lord! Wonderful is He in His love, His protection, and His divine work! Wonderful in each time He did say to one of His beloved: I am with you and will bring you back to the land.

2. Persons brought back to the land of the living through repentance:

The same words of the Lord may be taken spiritually as will be evident from the following examples:

* **St. Peter the apostle:** After denying the Lord Christ, he wept bitterly feeling that he became separated from the Lord and from His love, and from the other apostles, the ministry and the pastoral work. No doubt the words of the Lord that rang in his ears at that time were "*he who denies Me before men will be denied before the angels of God*" (Lk. 12: 9). However, the Lord comforted him with the same words He had previously said to our father Jacob, "*I am with you, and will bring you back*". But how did the Lord bring Peter back, and when? This happened when He appeared to him and said kindly, "*Feed My lambs ... Tend My sheep ... Feed My sheep*" (Jn. 21: 15-17). Only then did Peter feel that the Lord restored him to the apostles.

* **David the prophet**, committed adultery, killed, and fell from that high degree he had. And as if he had in mind the words of Origen [You, high tower, how did you fall?], he wept strongly and continually. Every night he used to wet his bed with his tears, but our good compassionate God did not leave him alone in his distress. He said to him, "*I am with you and will bring you back to the land*", '*I will bring you back to the land of repentance and purity, and reconciliation with God*'. And the Lord did bring David back, did wash him to be whiter than snow, and did restore to him the joy of his salvation (Ps. 51: 12).

A long time had passed when David thought he has no salvation, but he cried to the Lord, "*Lord, how they have increased who trouble me! Many are they who say of me: There is no help for him in God"* (Ps. 3). But amidst all these thoughts which Satan implants within us, there appear God's promises full of hope *"Behold, I am with you ... and will bring you back to the land"*.

* And **Samson** was restored by the Lord after his fall.

* **Solomon**, also, the son for David, was restored in the same way, as the Lord said to David about him, *"If he commits iniquity, I will chasten him ... But My mercy shall not depart from him, as I took it from Saul"* (2 Sam. 7: 14, 15).

These words are the strongest weapon for repentance and return.

The problems with many lies in that they think they could return to God by their own will power, their determination, and their true intention to return. They do not remember the divine hand in their return!

Believe me, if it is in the power of a sinner to return by himself to God, no one will return.

But one should cry out to God, *"Heal me, O Lord, and I shall be healed; save me, and I shall be saved"* (Jer. 17: 14). The Lord Christ Himself says clearly, *"Without Me you can do nothing"* (Jn. 15: 5).

The soul that is inclined to sin, the weak will, the wars of the devil, and the spiritual hindrances, all these detain man and fight to prevent him from returning to God. However, God's grace resist these hindrances, and the Lord's voice says compassion-ately to the sinner, *"Behold I am with you and will keep you ... and will bring you back to this land"*.

God says: I will bring you back to this land wherever you might have strayed, and however far or impossible salvation seems to you or to others, even though repentance appears impossible.

I am with you when Satan fights you with despair.

Whenever the opponent fights you, saying that sin has become your nature and not mere habit, and that you will not be able to forsake it because it has become attached to you more than your own skin and even flows within you more than blood in your veins, even when Satan says this to you, do not be afraid of him or of his thoughts. Say rather to him: **I will not return to God by myself, or by my own power, but it is God who will restore me** as He said, "*I am with you and will keep you ... and will bring you back to this land*". God will restore me, for what is impossible with men, is possible with God (Mk. 10: 27).

In His promises, God says to us:

"*I will give you a new heart and put a new spirit within you; I will take the heart of stone out of your flesh. I will put My Spirit within you and cause you to walk in My statutes, and you will keep My judgments and do them*" (Ezek. 36: 26, 27). He says also, "*Come now, and let us reason together, says the Lord, Though your sins are like scarlet, they shall be as white as snow*" (Isa. 1: 18). It is God who does all this and restores us.

* **The Lord restores us to His land in many and various ways:**

He restores us by love and kindness, or by firmness and punishment, or sometimes by trials and tribulations. He may restore us by teaching and instructing or by patience and longsuffering. He restores us in any way, and by any means according to everyone's nature. In short He, by all means, saves some because He desires all men to be saved and to come to the knowledge of the truth (1 Tim. 2: 4). He has no pleasure in the death of the wicked, but that the wicked turn from his way and live (Ezek. 33: 11).

He is the compassionate shepherd who protects His

sheep.

He moves the hearts of people for you, and for you He ties up Satan so that he may not cause you any harm. He surrounds you from all sides so that you sing:

Praise the Lord, O Jerusalem!
Praise your God, O Zion!
For He has strengthened the bars of your gates.
He has blessed your children within you.
He makes peace in your borders,
And fills you with the finest wheat
(Ps. 147: 12-14)

It is God who strengthens the bars of your gates and makes peace in your borders.

Put always before your eyes God's work within your life, not your own work.

What does God do in your life? How does His hand work for you. His right hand works powerfully, it holds you and supports you.

What does the Holy Spirit do for you? How does God's power and the Lord Christ's grace work for you? How does the intercession of angels and prayers of saints help you?

Your own work comes in the second place, or rather the last place.

But God's work comes in the first place with His promise: *"I am with you and will keep you wherever you go, and will bring you back to this land"*

Would that this promise be kept in our minds!

Would that we put it always before our eyes that we may be comforted and strengthened. Remember these divine words whenever you fall in despair or think there is no salvation for you or that your struggle is useless.

Remember these words whenever Satan presses on you, deceiving you that you are in his hold.

Remember them when He says to you that he will not leave you and that you are in His hold. Say to Satan: Where is your hold? And what is your power? Where is the sting of death and the victory of Hades? (1 Cor. 15: 55). There is the divine promise "*I am with you and will keep you wherever you go*".

Yes God, I remember always Your words, but what about my brother Esau?

Esau is severe and cruel and threatens me, he once said in his anger, "*I will kill my brother Jacob*". But the Lord says, "*Do not fear ... I am with you and will keep you wherever you go*". Blessed are You, O Lord, and blessed is Your kindness. Let it be as You said.

Be strong within in spite of the troubles surrounding you.

Though the wicked plots secretly against you, though the waters flow around you, though people plot vain things and the rulers take counsel together against the Lord and against His anointed, saying: Let us break their bonds in pieces and cast away their cords from us ... take no heed in spite of all this, but rather put before you God's promise "*I am with you and will keep you wherever you go*"

True, my Lord, so long as You are with me, the whole world is nothing to me.

The whole world is vanity and grasping for the wind, or like the chaff which the wind drives away with all plots of the wicked, all uproar and noise of many waters, even with the deceit of Laban who changed the wages of Jacob ten times (Gen. 31: 7) and who gave him Lea instead of Rachel (Gen. 29).

So long, O Lord, as Your promise continues I will not fear

the Red Sea hindring me for You are capable of establishing a way for me in it to walk in while You be with me keeping me wherever I go.

Even though the Valiant Goliath defies me all the day and threatens me with his spear which is like the weaver's beam, or with his sword and his power and gloating, I will say to him: You come to me with a sword, with a spear, and with a javelin. But I come to you in the name of the Lord of hosts ... for the battle is the Lord's (1 Sam. 17: 45-47). I come to you with God's promise which says "*I am with you and will keep you wherever you go*"

That is why God's children are always happy and confident.

God's children have a peaceful heart throughout their spiritual struggling and spiritual wars. They never get wearied because of diabolic wars or struggling against the hosts of wickedness and the rulers of the darkness of this age. They do not care for the troubled and confused world surrounding them, holding to God's promise full of hope and comfort.

You also, in your spiritual warfares, in all your troubles and problems, do not take heed of the powers fighting you or hindering you. You should rather focus your thoughts and emotions in God's promises which encourage, support and comfort you.

How good, kind and compassionate You are indeed, my Lord!

How comforting are you promises to your children throughout their voyage in the alienation of this world! How effectively You work and give protection! How joyful are Your encouraging words to Your children!

Enemies multiplied many times around David the prophet to the extent that he once said, "*Those who hate me without a cause are more than the hairs of my head*" (Ps. 69: 4). However, in all his troubles and in spite of those many enemies, he says to the Lord, "*I have rejoiced in the way of Your testimonies ... I will meditate on Your precepts and contemplate Your ways. I will delight myself in Your statutes. I will not forget Your word*" (Ps. 119: 14-16).

What, O David, are those testimonies that comforted you in your trouble.

"They are so many", he says, "but one only satisfies me: that is the Lord's promise "*I am with you and will keep you wherever you go and will restore you to the land*". I do not need except this promise; for so long as You are with me, O Lord God, and so long as Your promises are in my mind, I will fear no evil even though I walk through the valley of the shadow of death (Ps. 23: 4). You will find me courageous, faithful and full of hope in Your promise. Indeed, O God, You are wonderful as You said to Manoah, Samson's father:

"*Why do you ask My name, seeing it is wonderful?*" (Jud. 13: 18).

It is wonderful indeed to see God's children on their way in life and God holding the hand of each of them, encouraging each one, saying, "*I am with you and will keep you wherever you go*"

The power of Christianity lies in that it does not rely on any human power but only on the divine promise: I am with you and will keep you ...

God says: I will keep you from the devils and from the wicked people. I will keep you even from yourself, and from all evil. I shall preserve your soul and preserve your going out and your coming in (Ps. 121). "*A thousand may fall at your side, and ten thousand at your right hand; but it shall not come near you*" (Ps. 91: 7), "*You shall not be afraid of the terror by night, nor of the arrow that flies by day, nor of the pestilence that walks in darkness"* (Ps. 91: 5, 6). Though you walk through the valley of the shadow of death, you will fear no evil. *"Do you know why?"* says the Lord, *"It is because I am with you -after death- and keep you wherever you go, and restore you to the land"*.

Let us contemplate now on the words:

3. I will restore you to the land:

We are a holy breath that came out of God's mouth to the earth where we began to live.

Our existence in the dust of the earth is considered a period of estrangement.

While in this body made of dust, and living on dust of the earth we cry out with st. Paul the apostle, *"Who will deliver me from this body of death"* (Rom. 7: 24). Then God will say to every one *"I am with you and will keep you wherever you go and will restore you to the land"*.

Which land does God refer to?

It is the land which st John the Visionary mentioned, *"Now I saw a new heaven and a new earth, for the first heaven and the first earth had passed away. Also there was no more sea"* (Rev. 21: 1).

Man looks amazed at this new land whose builder and maker is God (Heb. 11: 10), the holy land where there is no sin nor death, and no need of the sun or the moon to shine in it, for the glory of God illuminated it (Rev. 21: 23)

And God points at this land, saying, *"I am with you and will keep you wherever you go and will restore you to the land"* Blessed be the Lord's name now and forever and ever, Amen.

CHAPTER 8

WITHOUT ASKING

"For your heavenly Father knows that you need all these things

(Mt. 6: 32)

1. Without Asking:

One may exclaim how can one have hope though one does not pray or ask for God's grace, power, kingdom or righteousness? How can such a person attain salvation?

Salvation is for all people, as it is written, *"the Son of Man has come to seek and to save that which was lost"* (Lk. 19: 10). He seeks your salvation more than you seek it and without your asking for it. He always gives everything even if we do not ask.

It is delightful to receive from God what we asked for, but it is more delightful to receive without asking.

It is God's deep love and kind fatherhood to man which makes Him fully aware of what we need and gives out of His deep love not merely as a response to our prayers. This fact, my brethren, is established by many examples. I will mention some of these examples that you may have hope in God's work for you.

Since the beginning of creation, God's nature is demonstrated in His giving without anyone asking.

He gave existence to us without our seeking, and gave existence to all beings whether rational or irrational without being asked to do this. He created all from nothingness which has no mind to ask for anything.

God created us in His own image and likeness without being asked.

Even if the impossible is supposed and we had been able to ask to be created in a certain image, we would have not asked for His own image and likeness as He willed in His love to give us (Gen. 1: 26, 27).

Without being asked, God created nature for us and gave us dominion over it.

He prepared everything before creating us. He stretched out heaven as a ceiling for us, and paved the earth that we may be able to walk on it. As st. Gregory said in the Holy Mass he wrote: [You made me lacking nothing of the works of Your honor ... For me You silenced the sea. For me You tamed animals ...]. For us God created trees and fruits, plants and seeds, flowers and birds ... For us He made the light and the celestial laws ... though we did not ask for that. Not only this, but He also said to us in His love, *"be fruitful and multiply; fill the earth and subdue it; have dominion over the fish of the sea, over the birds of the air, and over every living thing that moves on the earth."* (Gen. 1: 28)

God made Eve for Adam without Adam asking for that!

God knew that Adam had no helper comparable to him like the other beings *(Gen 2: 20)*, so He created Eve for him. Thus people multiplied and filled the earth and dwelt on it without anyone asking for that.

It is God's way as a Loving Father and a Good Shepherd.

He does not wait till His children or His folk or creation ask to give them. He gives by His own initiative what they do want even though they do not ask anything.

Indeed, how can a small child know what he needs to ask for it?

But a father knows and is always aware of what his child wants and he gives his child without being asked to do. The same with our heavenly Father who is always aware of what we need, and as a loving Father He provides the needs of everyone, and of peoples and groups. He does not wait till they ask, for perhaps they will ask for things not for their benefit or the benefit of those around them!!

A priest visits the congregation and fulfills their needs without being asked, how rather more does God the chief High Priest and Shepherd of all shepherds!

Truly, how rather more is God *"the Shepherd and Overseer of (our) souls"* (1 Pet. 2: 25), who said in His compassion, *"I will feed My flock, and I will make them lie down. I will seek what was lost and bring back what was driven away, bind up the broken and strengthen what was sick"* (*Ezek. 34: 15, 16*)

He tends His people out of His love, not waiting till anyone draws His attention to that. However, we do ask because asking makes us feel familiarity as children to God and gives us inner joy when having our needs fulfilled. That is why the Lord said to His disciples, *"Until now you have asked nothing in My name. Ask, and you will receive, that your joy may be full."* (*Jn. 16: 24*)

It is the joy of being responded to, or of the feeling of familiarity, that makes us ask.

God gives us everything even if we do not ask. This fact is established by many examples in the Holy Bible which give us comfort and continuous hope in God who works for our happiness as a Father, a Shepherd and a Creator.

Lot was saved twice by God without asking to be saved

The first time God saved Lot when he was taken as a captive with the people of Sodom in the war between the four kings and the five kings (*Gen. 14*). Lot did not ask, but God moved the heart of his uncle Abraham and Abraham took his trained men and saved Lot and his house and the whole city.

The second time was when God decided to burn Sodom,

and Lot asked nothing, but God sent two angels to bring Lot and his family forcibly out of the city though Lot was lingering (*Gen. 19: 16*). God's compassion and mercy willed to save him.

God does not wait till man cries out to Him, for He says:

"For the oppression of the poor, for the sighing of the needy, now I will arise ... I will set him in the safety for which he yearns"

God did not say "For their prayers and supplications", but He said *"for the oppression ... for the sighing"*. Whether they ask or not the Lord rises and saves .... Each time God sees the oppression and sorrows of His people (*Ex. 3: 7*), He sends someone to save them as He did in the days of Moses and Gideon (*Judg. 6*). He saved Isaac at the last moment from being slaughtered, while the knife was on his neck though Isaac did not ask that (*Gen. 22*).

God gives everything good to every living thing without being asked to do.

He sends rain and sun and gives food to every living being even to the atheists who ask nothing from Him. He gives beauty to the lilies of the field, and gives good to all, not because they deserve it or ask for it, but because of His goodness and love.

Let us remember some of the great gifts God gave us:

2. God's Great Gifts:

* **An example of this is the holy Virgin bearing the Word God.**

Do you think that the holy Virgin asked for such a gift? Certainly not! It certainly did not occur to her, as she said to the angel, *"How can this be?!"*(*Lk. 1: 34*). But God gave her this great gift; the Mighty did great things for her (*Lk. 1: 49*) though she had not asked.

* **Redemption and salvation by the cross is another example for a gift not sought by man**

The first promise of salvation was given to man by God without man asking for it, when God said to man that the woman's seed would bruise the serpent's head (*Gen. 3: 15*). This way of salvation had never occured to man, not even in a dream.

Has ever anyone thought that God would become Man for our sake, empty Himself, suffer and die on the cross? When st. Peter the apostle heard this from the Lord Christ, he began to rebuke Him, saying, *"Far be it from You, Lord"* (*Mt. 16: 22*). No one ever asked the Lord to do this, but He did it for our salvation in spite of not being asked.

* **God's great gifts in His taking Elijah and Enoch up into heaven.**

Had Enoch ever dreamt or thought of being the first man taken by God into heaven? (*Gen. 5: 24*). Or had Elijah asked God to take him up by a chariot of fire into heaven? (*2 Kgs. 2: 11*). They are gifts that never occured to one's mind and never asked for by anyone. They are given by God to any of His children He wills to give to.

* **The eternal life is also a great gift from God.**

It is written about this eternal life, *"Eye has not seen, nor ear heard, nor have entered into the heart of man the things which God has prepared for those who love Him"* (*1 Cor. 2: 9*). Since these things are not known by man, how can one ask for them? Perhaps we would ask for happiness, but not in such a form. It is beyond our request. Everything in it no eye has ever seen nor ear ever heard, yet we receive it without asking.

* Did st. Paul the apostle ask to go up into Paradise (the third heaven)? Certainly not!

But Paul did see himself there in the body or out of the body, he knew not! Or did he ask to hear inexpressible words which no man should utter? Surely not! No one can ask for this.

3. Visions & Dreams:

Even visions were given people without their request.

Has our father Jacob ever asked to see a ladder reaching to heaven?!

Or has he asked to see the angels of God ascending and descending on the ladder and God's voice talking to him and comforting him *(Gen. 28: 12-15)*?! All this happened after he had deceived his father and obtained the blessing with deceit! Has not God given this vision to Jacob though Jacob did not ask?

The same happened for st. John when he saw the vision on the island called Patmos.

St. John never asked in his exile to see the Lord Christ with His eyes like a flame of fire and His countenance like the sun shining in its strength *(Rev. 1: 12-17)*. St. John could not even bear His vision and he fell at the feet of Christ as dead. He never asked to see heavens open and the Throne set and God on the Throne, the twenty four elders sitting around, the four living creatures, the seven angels with the trumpets and with the bowls of the wrath of God, and everything that was o happen. How would he have asked such a thing which he had not known about!

The same applies to the visions of Daniel & Ezekiel the prophets and all other visions, holy dreams and prophecies.

It is all a kind of divine revelation that no one could ever ask for since no one knows it or it ever occures to one mind.

The dreams of Joseph the righteous about his future life have never occured to his mind.

It never occured to him -being the youngest of his brothers- that his brothers and parents would come and kneel before him. How could he know that he might ask to see such a dream of the sun and moon and eleven stars bowing to him, or the sheaves of his brothers bowing down to his sheave (*Gen. 37*)!! This leadership God bestowed on Joseph and announced to him without Joseph seeking it.

The same can be said about Joseph's gift of interpreting dreams.

That is the case with every gift given man by God such as: the gift of playing music and compiling the psalms which God gave to David the prophet without asking (*1 Sam. 16: 18*), the gift of physical strength granted Samon without asking, the handsome form and appearance given Joseph (*Gen. 39: 6*), and the many gifts to Moses.

The holy dreams are also gifts by God for spiritual purposes.

Some dreams are given to grant some information, others for saving, comforting or announcing something. Joseph the carpenter was given the dream to be saved with his family from the sword of Herod (*Mt. 2: 13*). Another dream was given to the wise men from the east as a warning (*Mt. 2: 12*). The dreams given to Pharaoh were a warning for him to be prepared for the coming famine (*Gen. 41: 17-36*). The dream of Abimelech was to save Sarah the wife of Abraham (*Gen. 20: 3*), and Solomons' dream was to receive a blessing from the Lord God (*1 Kgs. 3: 5*). The dream of Nebuchadnezzar was interpreted by Daniel that he might be humbled and repent (*Da. 4: 4-27*). There are also the dreams announcing the birth of some persons such as the dream to Joseph the carpenter of the birth of the Lord Christ.

All these dreams no one asked for.

Visions and dreams are given by God as a gift of His Holy Spirit, the same as prophecies. God said in the Book of Joel the prophet, "*I will pour out My Spirit on all flesh; your sons and your daughters shall prophesy, your old men shall dream dreams, your young men shall see visions*" (*Joel 2: 28*). The same words are repeated in the Book of the Acts (*Acts 2: 17*).

Prophecies were given to the prophets though they had not asked for them.

Prophecies were given for our benefit without asking, and the prophets sent by God had never thought that they would be prophets. But in an unknown moment we hear words like "*The word that came to Jeremiah from the Lord..*"(*Jer. 7: 1*); "*The word of the Lord came expressly to Ezekiel*"(*Ezek. 1: 3*), "*The word of the Lord which came to Zephaniah*" (*Zeph. 1: 1*). All such words no one ever asked to hear.

Evidently the Lord speaks to people whenever He wills without being asked to do.

He gives a dream, a vision, a prophecy, or a gift whenever He wills in a time we never expect.

The gifts of the New Testament are far more marvelous:

4. Gifts of the New Testament:

No one ever dreamt of having such gift as: justification, regeneration, sanctification, and other gifts of the holy baptism, for st. Paul the apostle says, *"whom He called, these He also justified; and whom He justified, these He also glorified"* (Rom. 8: 30). We feel amazed at the words of the apostle:

"For as many of you as were baptized into Christ have put on Christ" (Gal. 3: 27)

He says also, *"Do you not know that your bodies are members of Christ?"* (1 Cor. 6: 15). Who ever can have asked or just thought that his body be a member of Christ's body or to put on Christ?! But God gives what we ask not for.

Who ever could have asked that his body be a temple of the Holy Spirit?

But the apostle declares this fact in (1 Cor. 6: 19) and repeats it in (1 Cor. 3: 16) *"Do you not know that you are the temple of God and that the Spirit of God dwells in you?"*. It is indeed a holy gift granted us by God. He gave us also the grace of being partakers of the Holy Spirit (Heb. 6: 4), and partakers of the divine nature (2 Pet. 1: 4), though we never asked for that.

Another gift given us is our becoming God's children.

"Behold what manner of love the Father has bestowed on us, that we should be called children of God" (1 Jn. 3: 1). We are also called Christ's brethren, *"He is not ashamed to call them brethren"* (Heb. 2: 11, 12).

A very marvellous gift given us is the Eucharist.

He gave us the Sacrament of Eucharist though we did not ask.

In an unexpected hour, the Lord Christ gave His disciples the Sacrament of Eucharist (*Mr. 26: 26-28*). He permitted us to eat His flesh and drink His blood so that we may abide in Him and have life in Him (*Jn. 6: 54-56*).

Would anyone have imagined such a gift! It is a free gift given unexpectedly like all other gifts God gives out of His all goodness without man asking for them.

5. God's Generous Giving:

The farthest dream of st. Elizabeth was to have a son, and perhaps she forget this request when she became old. Her husband Zacharias thought it has even become impossible, so he did not believe the angel who announced it to him (*Lk. 1: 18*) for time had elapsed when such a request would have been fulfilled.

But God gave Zacharias and Elizabeth the greatest of those born of women.

God granted them this great grace without their asking. He gave them His messenger who was to prepare His way before Him (*Mk. 1: 2*). He gave them one who was to be great in the sight of the Lord, to be filled with the Holy Spirit from his mother's womb, to go before Him in the spirit and power of Elijah (*Lk. 1: 15-17*). He gave them one of whom the Lord Christ said, *"more than a prophet"*, *"among those born of women there has not risen one greater than John the Baptist"* (*Mt. 11: 9-11*).

Neither Elizabeth nor Zacharias had asked for such a grace.

It is God's generous giving for He gives to all liberally

more than one seeks. Whatever we seek would be much lesser than God's generous giving and goodness.

A son is the only dream of a barren woman, but hear what the Lord says in the Book of Isaiah, *"Sing, O barren ... Enlarge the place of your tent, and let them stretch out the curtains of your dwellings ... For you shall expand to the right and to the left, and your descendants will inherit the nations, and make the desolate cities inhabited"* (Isa. 54: 1-3). All this He gives the barren even though she does not ask.

It might be a reference to the barren church of the gentiles who did not seek Him! Or perhaps it refers to any few number, or one desolate of virtues and barren of the work of the Spirit within!

Another example is the sinner struggling in her own blood mentioned in the Book of Ezekiel.

Probably that sinner sought only to be washed by the Lord to become clean, merely to repent and her repentance be accepted. But the loving merciful God says in His generosity, *"'I adorned you with ornaments ... and I put ... a beautiful crown on your head. You were exceedingly beautiful, and succeeded to royalty. Your fame went out among the nations because of your beauty, for it was perfect through My splendor which I have bestowed on you.' Says the Lord God"* (Ezek. 16: 11-14).

That sinner is a lesson in hope, for she who expected nothing received everything.

God is not ashamed of our being His children. If He finds our souls thrown out in our blood in the open field bare and hateful, He washes us and cleans us to remove our shame so we become His own, and He bestows on us His splendor and puts a beautiful crown on our heads. How great indeed is hope in God.

God does not give by measure; He gives plentifully and liberally. He opens for us the windows of heaven and pours out such blessing that there will not be room enough for it (*Mal. 3: 10*). He does all this without being asked by us.

He does not only wash the sinner, but He makes him whiter than snow.

God did not only accept the prodigal son, but He also bestowed on him many gifts out of His love and compassion. He put a ring on his hand and sandals on his feet. He put the best robe on him and killed for him the fatted calf and all were merry for his return (*Lk. 15: 22, 23*). The son had not required anything like that, he even was thinking of saying to his father "*Make me like one of your hired servants*" (*Lk. 15: 19*). He did not dare to ask for anything, but his father gave him everything.

God gives out of His goodness and generosity to satisfy our needs not because we ask or deserve that.

It is this goodness and generous kindness of God that implants hope within our hearts in spite of our unworthiness. The Holy Bible is full of examples proving this, of which we mention one example as a proof.

Joseph the righteous had one request: to be freed from prison. But God not only did free him from prison but also made him the first minister in Egypt and the second man in the kingdom.

Had Joseph ever sought this or even dreamt of it? Certainly not. But God the Compassionate always gives without waiting for us to ask. The story of Joseph in fact raises hope in all hearts. Suffice to remember how Joseph became in a bad state, how he was sold as slave, imprisoned for a long time and was accused though innocent, and in spite of all this God gave him generously what had never occured to him.

God's generous gifts are evident in His wonderful promises.

God promised, *"I am with you always, even to the end of the age"* (*Mt. 28: 20*); *"For where two or three are gathered together in My name, I am there in the midst of them"* (*Mt. 18: 20*). God gives us all these comforting promises though we did not ask.

God's love appears also in His divine call.

6. God's Divine Call:

The Lord Christ gave His disciples the honor of apostolicity which they never asked for.

Was it possible that Peter and Andrew seek such an honor while being busy with fishing and nets?! Was it possible for Matthew to ask for it while in the place of tax-collecting?! And the other apostles as well never asked for such an honor as the Lord Himself declared to His disciples, *"You did not choose Me, but I chose you and appointed you that you should go and bear fruit, and that your fruit should remain"* (*Jn. 15: 16*).

The prophets did not ask God to have the power to prophesy, but they got it.

When David was still a young boy looking after the few sheep in the wilderness, he certainly did not think or ask to be the anointed of the Lord or to be chosen from among his elder brothers and from among the whole people to be God's prophet! God chose him though he did not ask.

Young Jeremiah who said, *"I cannot speak, for I am a youth"*, did he ever dream of becoming a prophet to the nations? Yet God has called him without asking.

Abraham the father of the fathers also never asked, but was called by God (*Gen. 12: 1*).

All the prophets likewise were chosen by God though they did not ask, as the apostle says, "*For whom He foreknew, He also predestined ... whom He predestined, these He also called*" (*Rom. 8: 29, 30*).

Another clear example is Saul of Tarsus who persecuted the church.

Did Saul ever think of becoming a disciple of the Lord Christ? Certainly not! He resisted Christianity violently, but the Lord Christ appeared to him on his way to Damascus, called him, and chose him as apostle for the nations. The Holy Spirit also said to the apostles, "*Now separate to Me Barnabas and Saul for the work to which I have called them*" (*Acts 13: 2*).

Ruth likewise never thought of being a grandmother to the Lord Christ!

Certainly this never occured to her as she was a foreigner and gentile! But God, who calls those things which do not exist as though they did (*Rom. 4: 17*), always gives hope to people.

Take Rahab also for an example, did she ever require to be a grandmother to the Lord Christ?

Probably the utmost thing that she required was her and her family's safety when Jericho was to be attacked. She never thought of being among God's people; this was too much for her to think of, how much rather was to be a grandmother to Christ! It certainly never occured to her even in a dream. God the Compassionate gives without being asked. We have only to believe in His love, His generosity and His care for us.

7. Giving and Faith:

The saints, being sure that God gives without asking, could not dare to ask for anything except God Himself.

David the prophet said in his prayers, *"Your face, Lord, I will seek. Do not hide Your face from me"* (Ps. 27: 8), *"One thing I have desired of the Lord, that will I seek: that I may dwell in the house of the Lord all the days of my life to behold the beauty of the Lord and to inquire in His temple"* (Ps. 27: 4). All other things are unimportant and the Lord will grant us without asking. This is what the Lord said expressly,

"Seek first the kingdom of God and His righteousness, and all these things shall be added to you" (Mt. 6: 33).

The Lord did not say: Ask for those things afterwards, but He said "these things shall be added to you", in other words God will give them to you without your asking. That is why all the supplications in the Lord's Prayer are spiritual, related to God's kingdom and righteousness. The other things are granted by God; for He knows that we do need them. As a Compassionate Father He knows the needs of His children and saves them the trouble of asking for them urgently.

However, God permitted the weak to ask whatever they want.

He said, *"Ask, and it will be given to you"* (Mt. 7: 7), ask and you will rejoice when given and your faith will grow, and when your faith grows you will then ask for nothing except God and His kingdom and righteousness. *"Ask and you will receive, that your joy may be full"* (Jn. 16: 24). God listens to your prayers and requests with His lovingkindness as if uttered by little children. Wonderful indeed is our loving God who responds to all supplications of His children.

One who trusts in God and in His giving rests peacefully in His bosom.

Such a person is always sure that God manages every thing, as Peter was in prison asleep and sure of God's action for him. He was so fast asleep that the angel who saved him had to strike him on the side and raise him up (*Acts 12: 7*). He was fast asleep though he knew that Herod was intending to kill him because he was sure that God is watching over his salvation. See also what David the prophet says in the psalm:

"The Lord is my shepherd; I shall not want"(*Ps. 23: 1*)

Since one wants nothing, one does not ask because God cares for everyone. So we say in the Holy Mass written by st. Gregory: [You left me wanting nothing of Your glorious works].

If God asks you: What do you want? Would you then answer Him:

O Lord, You have left nothing lacking to want it! If I spend my whole life thanking You, this will not be sufficient. You give me whatever You see that I need.

You, Lord, flooded Your gifts over me and gave me more than what I wanted. You left me lacking nothing, for You know my needs if ever I have any after Your giving. My duty is solely to thank and praise You for Your lovingkindness not to ask for anything.

Some would ask: What should we do in tribulations? We tell them that God's children who trust in His care and love never feel troubled or uneasy. They leave the matter in God's hand and this makes them comfortable.

No one loves man more than God, and no one cares for us

more than Him. So, if everything is in His hands nothing should be said or sought.

Suffice that we seek God's love because He want our hearts.

God does not force us to love Him, but wants us to love Him of our own will. If we lack the power to love we can ask Him for it and He will pour it in our hearts through His Holy Spirit. God does not frighten us by His divinity, but attracts us with His love and wants exchanged love. He says, *"My son, give Me your heart"* (*Prov. 23: 26*).

Whenever God's love reigns over the heart, one does not desire anything in the world.

In such a case one says to the Lord, *"There is none upon earth that I desire besides You"* (*Ps. 73: 25*), and repeats with st. Paul the apostle, *"Yet indeed I also count all things loss for the excellence of the knowledge of Christ Jesus my Lord ... that I may gain Christ and be found in Him"* (*Phil. 3: 8, 9*).

Let this be your only request: God, His love, His kingdom, and His righteousness, and it will be sufficient. Let your heart be filled with hope that God knows any other things you want and with His love and care will give you what you need.

CHAPTER 9

Hand With Us

God's hand with us is very necessary for many important reasons:

Among the reasons is the words of the Lord, *"Narrow is the gate and difficult is the way which leads to life, and there are few who find it"* (Mt. 7: 14). If it is so, the divine justice necessitates that we receive divine help by which we can get from the narrow gate. Therefore the Lord says,

"Without Me you can do nothing" (Jn. 15: 5).

If God's hand is not with us, we shall be completely incapable whether in our strife against sin, in our ministry for the kingdom, or in acquiring any virtue whatsoever.

We are not only requested to be holy, but also to be perfect.

The apostle says, *"As He who called you is holy, you also be holy in all your conduct, because it is written, 'Be holy, for I am holy'"* (1 Pet. 1: 15, 16). It is not only holiness that we should acquire but perfect holiness is required, for the Lord says, *"Therefore you shall be perfect, just as your Father in heaven is perfect"* (Mt. 5: 48). In order to attain such holiness and perfection, we should receive the divine help to carry us along the way.

Our enemy is strong, and his wiles are numerous and deceiving.

The apostle says about this enemy, *"your adversary the devil walks about like a roaring lion seeking whom he may devour. Resist him, steadfast in the faith"* (1 Pet. 5: 8, 9). What faith can we resist the devil with? It is the faith that when the devil fights us, he will be conquered by God. It is so written in the Book of Job, "*God will vanquish him, not man*" (*Job. 32: 13*). Yea, we cannot -without God's hand with us- conquer that sin which is said to have cast down many wounded, and all who were slain by her were strong men (*Prov. 7: 26*). We have then to wait for the divine help.

Our enemy is strong, and our nature is also weak.

David the prophet was aware of this fact, and talked much about the greatness of God's forgiveness as in (*Ps. 103: 14*) "*For He knows our frame; He remembers that we are dust*", and in (*Ps. 6: 2*) "*Have mercy on me, O Lord, for I am weak*". This weak nature is clear in the faults of the prophets which the Scriptures mentioned. If such great people fell, what would happen for us if not supported by God's hand! But certainly He stretches His hand to us as the apostle asserts,

"*where sin abounded, grace abounded much more.*" (***Rom. 5: 20***).

It is true, grace abounds to save us from sin. That is why David the prophet cried out to the Lord, saying, "*You knew my path. In the way in which I walk they have secretly set a snare for me. Look on my right hand and see, for there is no one who acknowledges me; refuge has failed me; no one cares for my soul. I cried out to You, O Lord: I said, 'You are my refuge, my portion in the land of the living. Attend to my cry ... Deliver me from my persecutors, for they are stronger than me'*" (*Ps. 142*). O Lord, protect me for they are strong and I am weak.

Ignorance, lust and weak willpower are human weaknesses.

Sometimes man cannot know the way leading to God or the means by which salvation can be attained. Therefore the psalmist says, "*Teach me Your statutes. Make me understand the way of Your precepts*" (*Ps. 119*); "*Cause me to know the way in which I should walk ... Teach me to do Your will*" (*Ps. 144*). He sings joyfully because God guides him, saying, *"Good and upright is the Lord; therefore He teaches sinners in the way. The humble He guides in justice"* (*Ps. 25*). So God interferes to guide man on the way.

Man may have the knowledge, but the will is weak.

Man may either refuse good because of his love of sin or because he cannot do good though he wants to. That is why st. Paul the apostle says, *"For I know that in me (that is, in my flesh) nothing good dwells; for to will is present with me, but how to perform what is good I do not find. For the good that I will to do, I do not do; but the evil I will not to do, that I practice. Now if I do what I will not to do, it is no longer I who do it, but sin that dwells in me"* (*Rom. 7: 18-20*).

God, therefore, works in man with His grace.

St. Paul the apostle ascribes every work he performs to God's grace working in him; he says, *"But by the grace of God I am what I am"*, *"yet not I, but the grace of God which was with me"* (*1 Cor. 15: 10*). He also sends to his disciple Timothy, saying *"You therefore, my son, be strong in the grace that is in Christ Jesus"* (*2 Tim. 2: 1*).

Due to the importance of grace, the father apostles began their Epistles with it.

In the Epistles of st. Paul, the words *"Grace to you and peace from God"* are repeated in the beginning, as in (Rom 1: 7; 1 Cor. 1: 3; 2 Cor.1: 3; Gal. 1: 3; Eph. 1: 2; Phil. 1: 2). St. Peter the apostle also starts his two Epistles with the words, *"Grace to you and peace be multiplied"* (*1 Pet. 1: 2*); *"Grace and peace be multiplied to you"* (*2 Pet. 1: 2*). St. John as well addresses the seven churches in the Book of Revelation by the words, *"Grace to you and peace from Him"* (*Rev. 1: 4*). St. John even distinguishes between the grace of the New Testament and what was obtained in the Old Testament by saying, *"For the law was* given through Moses, but grace and truth came through Jesus Christ" (Jn. 1: 17).

This grace is the power of God working with us and in us.

This grace worked also in the father apostles so they were able to perform their mission and witness to the Lord as the Book of Acts tells us, "*And with great power the apostles gave witness ... and great grace was upon them all*" (Acts 4: 33). The angel who came to st. Mary the Virgin hailed her with the words, "*Rejoice, highly favored one, the Lord is with you*" (Lk. 1: 28).

God works in us with His grace and with His Holy Spirit.

The Holy Spirit works with us, giving us power. So the Lord Christ said to His holy apostles, "*But you shall receive power when the Holy Spirit has come upon you; and you shall be witnesses to Me*" (Acts 1: 8).

The communion of the Holy Spirit thus has been a blessing given to the believers as st. Paul the apostle says in his Second Epistle to the Corinthians, "*The grace of the Lord Jesus Christ, and the love of God, and the communion of the Holy Spirit be with you all. Amen*" (2 Cor. 13: 14). And this is the same blessing the church gives her children at the end of every meeting.

Not only the communion of the Holy Spirit do we enjoy, but also the presence of the Lord Christ with us as He promised.

"*Lo, I am with you always, even to the end of the age*" (Mt. 28: 20).

This great promise gives us hope that the Lord will be with us all our days, for He says also, "*For where two or three are gathered together in My name, I am there in the midst of them*"

(*Mt. 18: 20*). This is evident from the Book of Revelation where the Lord is depicted in the midst of the seven churches with the shepherds of those churches on His right (*Rev. 1: 13, 16, 20*). Yea, the Son is with us, He works with us and in us. But what about God the Father? The Lord says:

"*My Father has been working until now, and I have been working*" (*Jn. 5: 17*).

God's work did not end when He completed the creation took rest on the seventh day! God works continually, He sees everything, and observes everything, being the Almighty. He takes care, supports, helps, protects and assists the people as we read about the father apostles, "*And they went out and preached everywhere, the Lord working with them and confirming the word through the accompanying signs. Amen.*" (*Mk. 16: 20*). And David the prophet said about God's work, "*O Lord, how manifold are Your works! In wisdom You have made them all*" (*Ps. 104: 24*).

The Holy Trinity works with us and His angels also do.

The apostle said of the angels, "*Are they not all ministering spirits sent forth to minister for those who will inherit salvation*" (*Heb. 1: 14*). This is true, for one of the seraphim flew with a live coal from the altar in his hand and touched with it the lips of Isaiah the prophet when he heard Isaiah saying, "*Woe is me, for I am undone! Because I am a man of unclean lips*" (*Isa. 6: 5-7*).

And the Angel of the Lord defended Joshua the high priest against Satan and said, "*The Lord rebuke you, Satan!*" (*Zech. 3: 2*). Time is lacking to talk about the work of angels for humans by the order of the Lord. Daniel the prophet for example said, "*My God has sent His angel and shut the lions' mouths*" (*Da. 6: 22*). And the angel saved Peter from the prison (*Acts 12*), It is also written, "*The angel of the Lord encamps all around those who fear Him, and delivers them*" (*Ps. 34: 7*). In our troubles

God works for us as it is said, *"In all their affliction He was afflicted and the Angel of His presence saved them"* (Isa. 63: 9).

God works for us in all our afflictions and temptations.

God says to each of us, *"I will not leave you nor forsake you... Be strong and of good courage; do not be afraid, nor be dismayed, for the Lord your God is with you wherever you go"* (Josh. 1: 5, 9). He said to Jeremiah the prophet, *"Do not be afraid of their faces, for I am with you to deliver you"* (Jer. 1: 8). And to st. Paul the apostle He said, *"Do not be afraid, but speak, and do not keep silent; for I am with you, and no one will attack you to hurt you"* (Acts 18: 9, 10).

Even when we speak God is with us speaking by our tongues.

This is what the Lord said, *"Do not worry about how or what you should speak. For it will be given to you in that hour what you should speak; for it is not you who speak, but the Spirit of your Father who speaks in you"* (Mt. 10: 19, 20). That is why st. Paul the apostle asked the Ephesians to pray for him that utterance might be given to him when he opens his mouth (Eph. 6: 19). David the prophet also asked God to open his lips and mouth to praise Him (Ps. 51), and the Lord God said to Jeremiah the prophet, *"Behold, I have put My words in your mouth"* (Jer. 1: 9).

If we contemplate on God's hand in our repentance we can say that it is God who works in us to repent, as Jeremiah said,

"Restore me, and I will return" (Jer. 31: 18).

It is God's Spirit who convicts us of sin (Jn. 16: 8), and guides us to righteousness. The Psalmist was aware of God's work for one's repentance, so he said, *"Purge me with hyssop, and I shall be clean. Wash me, and I shall be whiter than snow"*

(*Ps. 51*). And in the Holy Mass we pray, saying, [Cleanse our souls, our bodies and our spirits], for God, in baptism, gave us the washing of the second birth (*Tim. 3: 5*), and promised us of this washing in the Book of Isaiah (*Isa. 1: 18*) and in (*Ezek. 36: 25*). The words of the psalm that need some contemplation are:

"Create in me a clean heart, O God, and renew a steadfast spirit within me" (***Ps. 51***).

This means that the clean heart is God's work; He creates the heart from nothing and renews the spirit. This is clear from the words of the Lord in the Book of Isaiah, *"I will give you a new heart and put a new spirit within you ... I will put My Spirit within you and cause you to walk in My statutes, and you will keep My judgments and do them"* (*Ezek. 36: 26, 27*).

God desires that all men be saved and come to the knowledge of the truth (*1 Tim. 2: 4*).

He does not only want, but He works also for our salvation. He managed a way for redemption and atonement, and He emptied Himself and was incarnated. He so loved the world that He gave His only begotten Son that whoever believes in Him should not perish but have everlasting life (*Jn. 3: 16*).

God gave the apostles the ministry of reconciliation to reconcile us to Him.

Thus says st. Paul the apostle, *"... God, who has reconciled us to Himself through Jesus Christ, and has given us the ministry of reconciliation ... How then we are ambassadors for Christ, as though God were pleading through us: we implore you ... be reconciled to God"* (*2 Cor. 5: 18, 19*).

God also said, *"Behold I stand at the door and knock"* (Rev. 3: 20).

God knocks at the door of each one and seeks the salvation of every soul as He did for the last sheep and the lost coin (*Lk. 15*). For this salvation He sent the prophets, the apostles, the shepherds and the teachers, and He sent us His words through the divine revelation.

God's work for us appears also in His protection to us.

For this the psalmist sang, *"If it had not been the Lord who was on our side, when men rose up against us, then they would have swallowed us alive ... Blessed be the Lord, who has not given us as prey to their teeth, Our soul has escaped as a bird from the snare of the fowlers"* (*Ps. 124*). David said also to Goliath, *"the battle is the Lord's, and He will give you into our hands"* (*1 Sam. 17: 47*). Moses the prophet was sure of God's hand with them, so he said, *"Stand still, and see the salvation of the Lord ... The Lord will fight for you and you shall hold your peace"* (*Ex. 14: 13, 14*).

The devil wants us to fall in despair by making us forget God's work for us.

It is easy, however, to resist the devil. If he says to us that the Lord's way is difficult, we can reply: Suffice that God is with us in it! God turns difficult things easy. If the devil tries to convince anyone that he does not desire repentance, one should say: Suffice that God wants it and He will certainly lead us to it. And if the devil frightens us by the many enemies, we should say that those on our side are much more than them who are against us.

God works for us, but we have to respond to His work and have communion with Him.

That is why the apostle says, *"Today, if you will hear His voice do not harden your hearts"* (*Heb. 3: 8*). God works, but we should take part in His work. He sends His Holy Spirit to strengthen and guide us, but we should have communion with the Holy Spirit.

In this way, salvation become an outcome of God's work within us, our acceptance of such work, and our communion with the Holy Spirit through the means of grace.

This creates hope within us, but one may wonder how one asks God repeatedly for something and receives no response! One may wonder how, after request, the affliction continues and God does not interfere! Where is hope then? To such a person the psalmist says:

"Wait on the Lord. Be of good courage, and He shall strengthen your heart. Wait, I say, on the Lord" (*Ps. 27*).

CHAPTER 10

Wait For The Lord

Undoubtedly God works, in silence, for all His creation as a good Shepherd who wills good for all.

However, when people are in trouble and God's response delays, they think He does not work!

While thinking God is not working, God is deeply in work for them. They are not aware of this and need to wait till they see God's work or rather the consequences of God's work. They need to wait till they see with their eyes what they should have believed by faith. *"Wait on the Lord. Be of good courage, and He shall strengthen your heart. Wait, I say, on the Lord"* (Ps. 27).

How should we wait?

Who waits for the Lord should wait in hope, with a heart full of faith and trust, with no doubt, no trouble, no confusion, nor weary. One should wait with trust that the Lord will interfere and will work, and that everything will turn to good, as the apostle says:

"All things work together for good to those who love God" (*Rom. 8: 28*).

The Scriptures describe to us the great hope for those waiting for the Lord, *"But those who wait on the Lord shall renew their strength; they shall mount up with wings like eagles, they shall run and not be weary, they shall walk and not faint"* (*Isa. 40: 31*). The strength shaken by affliction shall be renewed through hope by waiting on the Lord, as the psalm says, *"your youth is renewed like the eagle's "* (*Ps. 103: 5*). Therefore one should wait on God with a strong heart full of faith and confidence in Him.

One should be confident that God will act and His action will be clear and powerful, but it will come in the suitable time, in a suitable fruitful way.

It is not meet to fix a certain time or certain means for God to act. Did He not say, *"It is not for you to know times or seasons which the Father has put in His own authority"* (*Acts 1: 7*). It is sufficient to put your problem in God's hand and forget it there trusting that He will solve it, no matter when. It is not your business, you have only to wait till God solves it in due time.

Basis for waiting:

1. Your waiting in hope should be based on trust in God's love to you.

You should trust that God loves you more than you love yourself, and He works for your good more than you can do for yourself. God desires all men to be saved and to come to the knowledge of the truth (*1 Tim. 2: 4*). He has inscribed you on the palms of His hands and kept you in His right hand, saying, *"I will not leave you nor forsake you"* (Josh. 1: 5).

2. Your waiting in hope should be based on trust in God's wisdom.

You should trust His unlimited wisdom which is beyond your thinking or any human thinking. His wisdom knows what is good because He sees everything evin that which you cannot see. Job the righteous became finally aware of this wisdom, so he said, *"I have uttered what I did not understand, things too wonderful for me, which I did not know"* (Job 42: 3). Be sure then that God manages your affairs with His wisdom whether you understand it or not. Deliver your heart to His wisdom and wait.

3. Your waiting in hope should be based on trust in His promises:

You should trust in the promises God said, *"I am with you always, even to the end of the age"* (Mt. 28: 20); *"Can a woman forget her nursing child ... Surely they may forget, yet I will not forget you"* (Isa. 49: 15); *"I have inscribed you on the palms of My hands"* (Isa. 49: 16); *"Be strong and of good courage ... for the Lord your God is with you wherever you go"* (Josh. 1: 9); *"No man shall be able to stand before you all the days of your life"* (Josh. 1: 5); *"I am with you, and no one will attack you to hurt you"* (Acts 18: 10).

Seeking Human Ways:

Who loses hope in waiting the Lord might seek human ways such as depending on one's own intelligence or cunning. An example of this is Rebekah who sought a human solution when she thought that Jacob would lose the promised blessing (Gen. 25: 23) and encouraged Jacob to deceive his father Isaac (Gen. 27).

Our father Abraham also, losing hope, sought a human solution by taking Hagar to beget him a son, and again took Keturah as a wife to beget him children (Gen. 25: 1). But all these solutions were refused by God.

Some, losing hope, may seek the counsel of magicians and diviners or seek the counsel of dead persons!!

Such matters were considered by God abominations of the nations, as He said, *"you shall not learn to follow the abominations of those nations. There shall not be found among you anyone who makes his son or his daughter pass through the fire, or one who practices witchcraft, or a soothsayer, or one who interprets omens, or a sorcerer, or one who conjures spells, or a medium, or a spiritist, or one who calls up the dead. For all who do these things are an abomination to the Lord"* (*Deut. 18: 9-12*). All such ways are human ways rejected by God, some of which are even diabolic ways.

Some other ways are hypnotism and fortunetelling by various ways (reading the lines drawn in a coffee cup, reading the lines on the hand palm, ... etc!)

God wants you to be led solely by Him, and to take your knowledge from Him. That is why David the prophet used to sing that his salvation is from the Lord or that the Lord Himself has become his salvation. But amazing indeed is that some of those who seek such abominable ways comfort themselves or the others by saying that such things come within the scope of science and the church cannot resist science!!

How can it be that God says in the Scriptures that calling up the dead is abomination hated by Him, while some say that it is a science and the church should not resist science?!

Even if such a matter is science, it is abomination hated by the Lord. God hates even magic and says *"You shall not permit a sorcerer to live"* (*Ex. 22: 18*); *"But the cowardly ... sorcerers, idolaters ... shall have their part in the lake which burns with fire and brimstone*" (*Rev. 21: 8*). Some say that there is a certain kind of magic -which they call white magic- which is acceptable! But there is no mention at all in the Scriptures of such a kind!

You should not seek such ways but rather wait for the Lord. Even though He tarries, do not go to sorcerers or the like.

Such ways demonstrate failure and despair or impatience and disdain of God's express command in (Deut. 18). When king Saul sought such ways God tore the kingdom from him and he died (1 Sam. 28). So, obey God's express command and never seek such wrong ways even if you think He lingered. But some might inquire how long we should wait.

How long should we wait?

God never delays. Delay is relative, differing from one person to another according to one's feeling. So when you say with the psalmist, "*O Lord, do not delay*" (*Ps. 70: 5*), it means: Do not let me feel, O Lord, that you have delayed.

God works calmly and wisely while we think it slowness.

All God's works are done in the proper time, not slowly nor in haste. The timing is accurately fixed by God's astonishing wisdom.

God gave Adam and Eve the promise of salvation, but thousands of years passed and the promise was not fulfilled.

God said that the seed of the woman will bruise the head of the serpent. But thousands of years passed and the serpent remained with its head high! On the contrary, the seed of the woman began their downfall and God sent the flood to drown the whole world, destroyed Sodom with fire, and ordered the earth to open its mouth to swallow Korah, Dathan and Abiram, but God's promise remained.

Even though that seed of the woman perished, no matter. There is still hope in another seed that will come for salvation.

Hope once concentrated in Noah's children. When most of them became corrupt, hope moved to Abraham's children, then to Jacob's children. By all means God fulfills His promise of salvation. Though Simon the elderly waited long, but time came when he carried the Lord Christ and said, *"Lord, now You are letting Your servant depart in peace, according to Your word; for my eyes have seen Your salvation"*(Lk. 2: 29, 30). Even the Samaritan woman, in spite of her many sins, never lost hope in the coming of Christ. That is why she said, *"I know that Messiah is coming (who is called Christ). When He comes, He will tell us all things"*(Jn. 4: 25).

Many departed before witnessing salvation, but they departed in hope.

As st. Paul the apostle says, *"These all died in faith, not having received the promises, but having seen them afar off were assured of them, embraced them and confessed that they were strangers and pilgrims on the earth"*(Heb. 11: 13). These sang with the Psalmist, *"For You will not leave my soul in Sheol, nor will You allow Your Holy One to see corruption"*(Ps. 16: 10).

Here we would like to ask an important question:

Has God actually delayed in fulfilling His promise of salvation to the world?

Nay. He has not delayed though thousands of years passed.

He was preparing humanity to accept such salvation through prophecies, repentance and faith. Many sacrifices and burnt offerings were offered by them till the atonement and redemption dogma became implanted in their minds, and forgiveness through blood acceptable to them ... God waited till all people could receive and accept faith, even the Gentiles ... God waited till John the Baptist came and prepared the way before Him ... God waited till the holy virgin came who alone could be the bearer of the Incarnate Word, and who could bear such great glory.

It was not then a delay but a step towards preparation in hope.

God never forgot His promise throughout thousands of years. He was only preparing for its fulfillment, and finally the woman's seed could bruise the serpent's head (Gen. 3: 15). Thus the words God said to our father Abraham, *"In your seed all the nations of the earth shall be blessed"*(Gen. 22: 18; Acts 3: 25).

God gave humanity salvation *"When the fullness of the time had come"*(Gal. 4: 4).

Wrong Understanding of Delay:

When we say *"Wait on the Lord"*, does it mean that we shall wait in trust till He starts work? Nay. This concept is fit for the human understanding. But what is the true meaning?

We should wait, trusting not that God will work but that He is actually working even before we ask.

There might be a church in need of a priest and asks the Lord for that. It might seem that God delayed for two or three years before sending the priest, but the fact is that God has been preparing the priest thirty or forty years ago before the church asks. God has been preparing the priest spiritually and providing him with knowledge, wisdom and training. God might even have prepared the required priest with temptations and tribulations, or with spiritual experience that he would be fit for the ministry in that church. We, on the other hand, not knowing God's dispensation or arrangement, think that He delayed in fulfilling His promises!

Reasons and wisdom behind the alleged delay:

1 - The delay might be a chance for you to strengthen and deepen your prayers and spiritualities.

Such a delay will probably cause us to pray strongly from all the heart, continually and relentlessly. We might also fast and be humiliated before God or give vows. Hanna, Samuel's mother, for example, was barren for God did not give her children at first and the other wife of her husband used to tease her, but Hanna *"prayed to the Lord wept in anguish. Then she made a vow"* (1 Sam. 1: 9-12). She promised God that the male child He will give her, she will give to the Lord all the days of his life. She made use of the so called delay, or we can rather say that God found that the suitable time to give her offspring was that time when she attained such spirituality.

2. The reason might be that the Lord is preparing a better way:

Had God responded to Joseph the Righteous since the beginning of his imprisonment, he would perhaps have been freed to serve Potiphar or any other master or to work in any other field. But the said "delay" was not delay but a period of waiting till Pharaoh dreamt his dream for which he found no interpretation, and till Pharaoh's chief butler told him about Joseph. Then Joseph interpreted the dream wisely and thus became the first minister of Egypt and a father to Pharaoh. In this way what seemed to be delay was in fact a preparation for a better status.

3. The reason might be to test our faith

It is a test for us whether we become worried when our prayers are not responded to immediately, whether we grumble, resort to a human being, complain to others, blaspheme, or we wait with faith, hope and trust? It is a test from God to our faith, and a test from us to ourselves so that we may be able to treat any weakness that may be found in us.

4. The reason might be to acquire a contrite heart.

The immediate response to every prayer might lead us to pride and vain glory. But such "delay" can lead us to humbleness and contrition so that we may be aware that we are very weak.

5. The reason might be to encourage us to reconcile with God.

When God "delays" in His response, we rethink the matter and see if God has not responded because of our sins. Then we remember the words of the Lord, "*Return to Me, and I will return to you*" (Mal. 3: 7). This would lead us to repentance, and such repentance would be the due time fixed by God without any delay.

6. The reason might be that we cannot know the value of the thing immediately obtained.

We may even give no thanks for such a thing. But if the response (delays) we will hold more to the request and feel how valuable it will be if realized. When the response comes after some time, our thanks will increase and we feel more His benevolence. This in turn would deepen our attachment to Him and would make us careful for what we got lest we lose it.

7. God may tarry during tribulation so that we may get its blessing.

In case God responds immediately and removes the tribulation, we shall not have the blessing we would get if the tribulation continued and we endured patiently. Moreover, we would obtain crowns besides spiritual experiences. We would also acquire the virtue of long suffering, submission to the Lord and waiting on Him.

8. The reason for what we think to be (delay) might be that God is preparing something better than that which we ask for. God does not give us merely what we asked for, but He gives us what suits and is of benefit to us.

God does not respond to the literal words of the prayer but to the spirit of the prayer. He knows our needs more than we know them, and knows what is best for us more than we know. Suffice to say to Him we need, and He will choose with His wisdom what is of benefit to us and conforms with God's holy will full of wisdom.

9. Perhaps the feeling that God delayed reveals that we do not know well to say "*Let Your will be done*"

We usually say this phrase in our prayer but probably we do not go into its depth, understand it or mean it. When the response to our request delays, we should say, 'O Lord, we are not imposing our will, but we just express what wishes and requests are within us. If You find them of benefit, may You grant them whenever You like, otherwise Let Your will be done, and we are fully satisfied.'

It is an exercise in the life of submission based on trust in God's dispensation

We have only to wait, with hearts full of peace and confidence, feeling that the whole matter has moved to God's hand and kind heart. This is sufficient.

CHAPTER 11

COMFORT THE FAINTHEARTED, UPHOLD THE WEAK

7KHVV

God the Compassionate

Truly God likes that a person be of strong personality, and to be strong in the spiritual life, in forbearance, in ministry, in understanding, and in everything.

However, God is God of the weak.

God upholds the weak, encourages them, strengthens them and never forsakes them. Of those the Lord Christ said, *"The spirit of the Lord God is upon Me, because the Lord has anointed Me to preach good tidings to the poor; He has sent Me to heal the brokenhearted, to proclaim liberty to the captives ... to comfort all who mourn ... to give them beauty for ashes, the oil of joy for mourning, the garment of praise for the spirit of heaviness"*(Isa. 61: 1-3).

Indeed, He supports these desperate, brokenhearted and mourning. We address Him as [**The hope of those who are hopeless and the help of those who have no helper; the comfort of the fainthearted; the harbor of those in the storm**]. He is the safe harbor to those in the ships tossed by the waves and storms like the disciples of the Lord in that stormy day. Their boat was in the middle of the sea tossed by the waves, and they saw Him walking on the sea, and as soon as He calmed them, saying, *"It is I; do not be afraid"*, the wind ceased (Mt. 14: 24-32).

Assuredly He is the help of those who have no helper.

He healed the man with infirmity for thirty eight years at Bethesda, who had no one to put him into the pool when the water was stirred up by the angel.

Whenever you feel alone and no one cares for you, you will

certainly find God on your side. Whenever you flee from the valiant Esau who wants to kill you, you will see a ladder between heaven and earth, and will hear God's voice calming you, *"Behold, I am with you and will keep you wherever you go"*(Gen. 28: 15). Whenever Pharao pursues you, even to the sea, and you feel mean-spirited, God will make a way for you in the sea. Do not be mean-spirited then, and if you feel that, listen to the words of the apostle, *"comfort the fainthearted, uphold the weak"*(1 Thess. 5: 14).

You also, if you see someone bewildered in despair and broken, do not disregard him. If you see one falling, do not despise him. Support, say an encouraging word, give hope, open a path to light the way of those. Brother, if you are on the top of the mountain, do not desdain those at the foot of the mountain or in the valley or even in the swamps. If God has given you a gift of grace and you attained a great status, do not look in contempt to those who have not yet attained or to the desperate and mean-spirited. Remember the words of the Lord:

"Take heed that you do not despise one of these little ones"(Mt. 18: 10).

Whatever bad condition those are in, God is capable of lifting them as He did to Augustine, Pelagia and Moses the Black. Even if a person is an unfruitful tree about to be cut down, the kind-hearted keeper of the vineyard wills to let it another year to dig around it and fertilize it for perhaps it will bear fruit (Lk. 13: 6-9). This is our good God.

"A bruised reed He will not break, and smoking flax He will not quench"(Mt. 12: 20).

The bruised reed might hold upright when supported, and the smoking flax might glow when blown. God gives the opportunity to everyone; for He has no pleasure in the death of one who dies but that he may turn and live (Ezek. 18: 23-32). So long as one is in this life one still has a chance for repentance and should not lose hope. The thief on the Lord's right believed at the last moment of his life on the earth and turned to God. He was a bruised reed that the Lord supported.

See what comforting words the Lord Christ says:

"I did not come to judge the world but to save the world"(Jn. 12: 47).

My mouth, He says, has no word of condemnation, but words of love, salvation and forgiveness. Moreover, any judgment against you, I will bear instead of you and blot it out with My own blood! Truly, Lord, Your mouth is most sweet and altogether lovely (Song 5: 16). Though all judgment is committed to You from the Father (Jn. 5: 22), You say: I did not come to judge.

Examples:

God sent the prophets a support to the weak, poor and falling humanity.

Though they rejected Him, He came to attract them. And when they had forsaken Him and hewn themselves broken cisterns that can hold no water (Jer. 2: 13), He did not forsake them but told them about the fountain of the living water. When they worshipped the gold calf, saying about it their god that brought them out of the land of Egypt (Ex. 32: 4), He did not destroy them. He rather turned from His fierce wrath and accepted the intercession of Moses on their behalf. He still has patience and forbearance, and still raises those who are bowed down and gives freedom to the prisoners (Ps. 145).

In your mean-spiritedness, you may get desperate of attaining salvation, but God never despairs of attracting

you!

He has come to seek and to save that which was lost (Lk. 19: 10). He sought the tax-collectors and sinners and sat at their tables, saying, "*I have not come to call the righteous, but sinners, to repentance*", "*Those who are well have no need of a physician, but those who are sick*"(Lk. 5: 31, 32). He praised the tax-collector who stood afar, not daring to raise his eyes to heaven, and preferred him to the Pharisee, thus the tax collector went down to his house justified (Lk. 18: 13, 14).

He forgave even the sinner woman who was caught in adultery, in the very act.

That woman was covered with shame and mean-spiritedness; the scribes and Pharisees wanted to stone her, but the Lord delivered her from their hands, and said to her, "*Neither do I condemn you; go and sin no more*"(Jn. 8: 3-11). He encouraged also the sinner woman who washed His feet with her tears and wiped them with the hair of her head. He preferred her to the Pharisee and said, "*her sins, which are many, are forgiven*"(Lk. 7: 37-47)

Knowing this kindness of God who encourages the faint-hearted, David the Prophet addressed Him in repentance: "**Wash me, and I shall be whiter than snow**"(Ps. 51: 7). The words "*whiter than snow*" show the extent of God's kindness to the sinners. This made the Psalmist praise God in the beautiful psalm, "*Bless the Lord, O my soul, and forget not all His benefits*"; "*As a father pities his children, so the Lord pities those who fear Him*"; "*He has not dealt with us according to our sins, nor punished us according to our iniquities. For as the heavens are high above the earth, so great is His mercy toward those who fear Him; As far as the east is from the west, so far He removed our transgressions from us ... For He knows our frame; He remembers that we are dust*" (Ps. 103: 10-14).

God does not only forgive our sins, but says also, *"Their sin I will remember no more"* (Jer. 31: 34)

He says about the repentant sinner, *"None of the transgressions which he has committed shall be remembered against him"* (Ezek. 18: 22); *"None of his sins which he has committed shall be remembered against him"* (Ezek. 33: 16). And the psalmist says, *"Blessed is he whose transgression is forgiven, whose sin is covered. Blessed is the man to whom the Lord does not impute iniquity"* (Ps. 32: 1, 2). The same words are repeated by st. Paul in his epistle to the Romans (Rom. 4: 8). St. Paul said also about the redemption, *"God was in Christ reconciling the world to Himself, not imputing their trespasses to them"* (2 Cor. 5: 19).

Let no one be mean-spirited because of one's sins but to remember that God will not impute them in case one repents.

In repentance God blots out our sins and remembers them no more, *"Though your sins are like scarlet, they shall be as white as snow"*(Isa. 1: 18); *"whiter than snow"*(Ps. 51: 7)

Take for example st. Peter the Apostle who denied the Lord Christ:

Peter did not only deny the Lord, but also, *"he began to curse and swear: I do not know this Man of whom you speak"*(Mk. 14: 71)(Mt. 26: 74). He forgot that he had said before to the Lord, *"Even if all are made to stumble, yet I will not be"*; *"If I have to die with You, I will not deny you"*(Mk. 14: 29, 31)(Mt. 26: 33, 35). Seeing himself denying Him thrice, he became fainthearted and went out and wept bitterly (Mt. 26: 75).

However, the Lord did not let His disciple be a victim of mean-spiritedness, but He encouraged him in many ways.

After the Resurrection, the Lord said to the Marys by the

mouth of His angel, *"But go, tell His disciples -and Peter- that He is going before you into Galilee; there you will see Him"* (Mk. 16: 7). He did not include Peter among the disciples, but mentioned him separately, because Peter was in need of special care to restore to him his peace after his denial of the Lord. And when the Lord Christ showed Himself to seven of the disciples at the Sea of Tiberias, he said to Peter, *"Do your love Me more than these? ... Feed My lambs ... Tend My sheep ... Feed My sheep"*(Jn. 21: 15-17). By these words the Lord meant to assure him that he did not lose his apostolic rank by denying the Lord. Moreover, st. Paul the apostle, telling about the Lord's apparitions after the Resurrection, said, *"He was seen by Cephas, then by the twelve"* (1 Cor. 15: 5).

The Lord did the same to Thomas when he suspected the Lord's Resurrection.

Thomas was too weak to believe without seeing. He alone did not believe whereas all the other disciples believed. So the Lord did not leave him in his suspicion and faint heartedness, He showed Himself to him and showed him His wounds. The Lord said to Thomas, *"Reach your fingers here and put it into My side. Do not be unbelieving, but believing"*. Thus Thomas believed and addressed the Lord, *"My Lord and my God"*(Jn. 20: 27, 28).

Let us see also how the lord God treated Moses who was slow of speech and slow of tongue (Ex. 4: 10)

Moses was aware of that weakness in himself and knew that he was not fit because of it. Therefore he said to the Lord God, *"I am not eloquent, neither before nor since You have spoken to Your servant"*(Ex. 4: 10); *"I am of uncircumcised lips, and how shall Pharaoh heed me?"* (Ex. 6: 30). However, God encouraged him and did not leave him in his mean-spiritedness.

This person of uncirmcised lips even became God's spokesman.

God said to Moses, *"Go, and I will be with your mouth and teach you what you shall say ... Is not Aaron the Levite your brother? ... Now you shall speak to him and put the words in his mouth. And I will be with your mouth and with his mouth, and I will teach you what you shall do ... And he himself shall be as a mouth for you, and you shall be to him as God"*(Ex. 4: 12-16).

God encouraged all the young and those who feared to shoulder responsibility.

When Jeremiah said to God, *"I cannot speak, for I am a youth"*, the Lord God said to him, *"Do not say: I am a youth ... Do not be afraid of their faces, for I am with you to deliver you"*. Then the Lord put forth His hand and touched Jeremiah's mouth and said, *"Behold, I have put My words in your mouth. See, I have this day set you over the nations and over the kingdoms, to root out and to pull down, to destroy and to throw down, to build and to plant"* (Jer. 1: 6-10). The Lord encouraged Jeremiah even more and said to him, *"For behold, I have made you this day a fortified city and an iron pillar, and bronze walls against the whole land ... they will fight against you, but they shall not prevail against you. For I am with you to deliver you"*(Jer. 1: 18, 19).

In the same way the Lord God encouraged Joshua after the death of Moses.

It was not easy for Joshua to fill the big space left by Moses the great prophet. This made him look down on himself. But the Lord God encouraged him, saying, *"No man shall be able to stand before you all the days of your life; as I was with Moses, so I will be with you. I will not leave you nor forsake you. Be strong and of good courage ... Have I not commanded you? Be strong and of good courage; do not be afraid, nor be dismayed, for the Lord your God is with you wherever you go*" (Josh. 1: 5-9).

The Monk's Paradise tells us this story about st. Anba Isizerus the priest supervising the monks, the story says:

Whenever a brother is dismissed by the fathers after failing to reform him, Anba Isizerus used to take him and treat him with much tolerance until he was cured. When Anba Moses the black came to the monastery and looked very fearful, they sent him to st. Isizerus who took care of him. But Anba Moses had a heavy load of sins at the beginning of his repentance to the extent that one night he went to his spiritual father Isizerus eleven times. When st. Isizerus advised him to stay in his cell, Anba Moses said that he was not able because bad thoughts pressed heavily on him. This tolerance by st. Isizerus made of Moses the black a saint.

Pieces of Advice:

Try always to keep up people's morale and spirit as the apostle says, "*uphold the weak*" (1 Thess. 5: 14). If you see someone rebuked, criticized by others and is humbled, try to embrace him and speak well on his behalf. Certainly such a person will never forget this nobility all his life. It is the duty of the great hearts filled with loving kindness towards the mean-spirited.

If you find someone bound up in sins, do not reproach him, but rather liberate him.

Do not do like that person who saw one day a youth struggling the waves and about to drown, and he began to reproach him, saying: O my son, since you do not know how to swim why did you go into the sea? And of course the youth answered him: Sir, may you save me from drowning then reproach me as you wish afterwards! Therefore, do not reproach anyone for failure, but give hope in success.

Do not say: I have given many advices but no use. You should rather have long-suffering.

Hearken to the apostle, saying, "... *uphold the weak, be patient with all*" (1 Thess. 5: 14). Overcoming a deep-rooted sin needs time and patience, so be patient with the weak until God's grace visits and delivers them. Remember that you also have a similar nature, and put before you the words of the apostle, "*Remember the prisoners as if chained with them -those who are mistreated- since you yourselves are in the body also*"(Heb. 13: 3).

Remember that those who discouraged the congregation were not allowed by God to enter into the promised land.

God prevented those who discouraged the congregation, saying, "*We are not able to go up against the people, for they are stronger than we ... There we saw the giants the descendants of Anak ... and we were like grasshoppers in our own sight*"(Num. 13: 31, 33).

Search for the good aspects of the life of a person - whether a sinner or a weak person- and reveal and praise them.

This is what the Lord Christ did for the Samaritan woman. In spite of her sins, the Lord said to her, "*You have well said: I have no husband ...*" "*In that you spoke truly*"(Jn. 4: 17, 18). This praise encouraged the woman to confess and He won her for repentance.

A person may be encouraged by a good word, another by a good example, by some story or verses from the Scriptures, by relieving him from the burden of sin, by telling him about God's grace and action, or even by ignoring many of his faults. In fact reproach for every fault might lead to despair.

CHAPTER 12

GOD TAKES THE INITIATIVE

The life of repentance and the relationship between God and man take one of two ways:

1. Man comes to God and God accepts him:

This conforms with God's true promise, *"the one who comes to Me I will by no means cast out"*(Jn. 6: 37). This is what happened to the prodigal son: When he became aware of his bad condition, he decided to go to his father, and when he went his father received him joyfully (Lk. 15: 17-24). God wants such repentance and turning as He says, *"Return to Me and I will return to you"* (Mal. 3: 7).

2. God starts the relationship with man:

In this case it is God who goes to the person seeking his salvation as He sought the lost sheep and having found it He laid it on His shoulders rejoicing (Lk. 15: 4, 5). God takes the initiative as clear from His words, *"Behold, I stand at the door and knock. If anyone hears My voice and opens the door, I will come in to him and dine with him, and he with Me"* (Rev. 3: 20).

In this chapter we shall concentrate on the second way: God takes the initiative.

A person may not start the relationship with God for many reasons:

* **Being overcome by one's own lusts may prevent a person from starting**

One may be overcome by one's own lusts may prevent a person from starting. One may be overcome by one's own lusts when the lust presses on him from within or fights him from outside. In this case the lust has its impact on him and he becomes enslaved to it, loves it, and is not willing to be liberated from it (Jn. 5: 6). But what should such a person do? Should he submit to despair and lose hope? Nay, for God certainly takes the initiative, visits that person knocks at his door and attracts him.

* Being occupied with many things away from God may prevent a person from starting.

Such concerns may not leave any time for worship as the Lord said to Martha, *"you are worried and troubled about many things. But one thing is needed"*(Lk. 10: 41, 42). A person who has no time for God, for praying, for reading and contemplating, or for ministry, needs a powerful hand to take him out of his involvements.

* Being ignorant, not knowing how to start may prevent one from starting

An example of this is the people of Nineveh, *"who cannot discern between their right hand and their left"*(Jon. 4: 11). For those God took the initiative and sent them Jonah the prophet to guide them. Another example is Saul of Tarsus who ignorantly persecuted the church (1 Tim. 1: 13). Therefore the Lord Christ appeared to him and attracted him; and when he was influenced by this and believed, he asked the Lord, *"What do You want me to do"* (Acts 9: 6). This phrase was said also by the rich young man (Mt. 19: 16) and by the Jews on the Day of Pentecost (Acts 2: 37) as well as by many others.

* Being weak may prevent one from starting.

A weak person says, *"the evil I will not to do, that I*

practice"; *"the will is present with me, but how to perform what is good I do not find"*; *"But I see another law in my members, warning against the law of my mind, and bringing me into captivity to the law of sin ..."*; *"O wretched man that I am! Who will deliver me from this body of death?"* (Rom. 7: 18-24). Here God takes the initiative and saves such a person.

One may wonder: if one is not able to start, would God start?

Yes brother, God is ready to start. It is His way always, and the Holy Scriptures contain various examples where God took the initiative since Man's creation and even before that. Let us meditate on all of this.

A certain fact recorded in the Holy Scriptures is that:

God's relationship with man has been initiated by God.

* The relationship between God and man started when God created man; for had He not created man there would have been no such relation. Moreover, God created man in His own image after His likeness and gave him the spirit by which he can establish a relationship with his God.

* Not only did God create man, but He also initiated a relationship when man fell.

Man did not resort to God to confess his sin and ask His forgiveness and reconciliation. He rather escaped from God and hid behind a tree, but God came to him, talked with him and encouraged him to confess. God even promised to give him salvation when He said to him that the seed of the woman would bruise the head of the serpent (Gen. 3). It was as if God was saying to Adam: Are you afraid of me, Adam? Do not fear - I am going to reconcile with you. Are you terrified from sin and its results? Do not fear, I will forgive you and prepare for you the way of salvation.

* **No doubt it was God who started preparation for such wonderful salvation.**

It was God who taught the human beings the redemption and propitiation dogmas and that an innocent sinless soul should die for a sinful soul deserving death. It was He who gave man the rules concerning sacrifices and burnt offerings, and concerning uncleanliness and purification, and granted us repentance to life (Acts 11: 18).

* **It was God who started through inspiration and sent us the prophets.**

The aim of all this was to teach and guide us, and to convey to us His word. He gave the apostles the ministry of reconciliation (2 Cor. 5: 18) as st. Paul the apostle says, *"we are ambassadors for Christ, as though God were pleading through us: we implore you on Christ's behalf, be reconciled to God"* (2 Cor. 5: 20). It is God then who starts the reconciliation and sends His apostle to prepare for it.

* **God became incarnate and descended to us to redeem and save us.**

Before that we had no idea about incarnation and redemption and we had not asked for that. But God, by this wonderful salvation, has revealed His love towards us, *"For God so loved the world that He gave His only begotten Son, that whoever believes in Him should not perish but have eternal life"* (Jn. 3: 16).

Through the call God His relationship with man started.

The start was a call, whether to prophecy, apostolicity or priesthood. God called our father Noah and commanded him to make an ark to go and to go into it with his family to be saved and to keep the life of every creature (Gen. 6-8). The ark in the water was a symbol of baptism *"in which a few, that is, eight souls, were saved through water. There is also an antitype which now saves us - baptism"*(1 Pet. 3: 20, 21).

God called also our father Abraham -as He did to Noah- to make him a people taking the way of salvation.

It was God, not Abraham, who initiated the relationship; for God called Abraham to follow Him to the land that He showed him. Then God blessed Abraham and said to him, *"in you all the families of the earth shall be blessed"* (Gen. 12: 1-3); *"In your seed all the nations of the earth shall be blessed"* (Gen. 22: 18). The same promise was given by God to our father Jacob when He said to him, *"in you and in your seed all the families of the earth shall be blessed"* (Gen. 28: 14).

The blessing has been God's initiative.

Since the beginning, God granted the blessing to our forefathers Adam and Eve (Gen. 1: 28). Then He gave the same blessing to our father Noah and his children (Gen. 9: 1), to our father Abraham (Gen. 12: 12; 22: 17, 18), to our father Isaac (Gen. 26: 24), and to our father Jacob (Gen. 28: 14). The greatest blessing was the coming of Christ from their seed, in whom all the nations of the earth got the blessing through the salvation He gave the world. Salvation is indeed the greatest gift initiated by God and perfected by His love to man because He, *"desires all men to be saved and to come to the knowledge of the truth"* (1 Tim. 2: 4.)

For this salvation, God called the prophets and apostles.

* He called Moses the Prophet when He spoke to him from the midst of the bush (Ex. 3: 4) to send him to save His people. Moses never thought at that time of such a call or of seeking to save the people. He even execused himself more than once (Ex.

4: 10, 13).

* God called some people from their mothers' wombs.

He said to the young Jeremiah, *"Before I formed you in the womb I knew you; before you were born I sanctified you; I ordained you a prophet to the nations"* (Jer. 1: 5). John the Baptist also was said by the angel, *"He will also be filled with the Holy Spirit, even from his mother's womb."* (Lk. 1: 15). The same happened with our father Jacob (Rom. 9: 1-13) (Gen. 25: 23). And st. Paul the Apostle said about his call, *"But when it pleased God, who separated me from my mother's womb and called me through His grace ..."* (Gal. 1: 15). When the time came, God took the initiative again; He met st. Paul on the way to Damascus in shining light and called him (Acts 9).

It was the Lord Christ who called all the apostles and said to them, *"You did not choose Me, but I chose you ..."* (Jn. 15: 16), *"and appointed you that you should go and bear fruit, and that your fruit should remain"*. He chose His twelve disciples (Mt. 10: 1) and the seventy as well (Lk. 10: 1). Neither Peter nor Andrews had thought to follow Christ for they were involved in fishing. Matthew also never thought to be a disciple to Christ for he was working at the tax office. The same applies to the rest. However, the Lord started the relationship and called each of them, *"For whom He foreknew, He also predestined ... these He also called"* (Rom. 8: 29, 30). It is He who calls you when you are not aware for expecting this call. He says to you 'Come, follow Me', and leads you on the way, giving you strength, provided only that your heart is ready.

The Lord's apparitions to His disciples after the Resurrection give us a good idea about that God who always takes the initiative.

* After the resurrection, the Lord used to go to His disciples not they went to Him. A beautiful thing worth contemplation is that He came to them in the upper room when the doors were shut and they were assembled (Jn. 20: 19).

Have you ever experienced the Lord Christ penetrating the shut doors to speak to you?

It is reasonable and believable that the Lord speaks to us when we open to Him our doors (Rev. 3: 20). But to come and speak to us while the doors are shut is an amazing thing that He alone can do in His love. As for the apostles, the doors were shut because of fear not because of rejection ...

The Lord appeared also to His disciples while occupied with material matters.

The last chapter of the Gospel according to st. John tells us that the Lord appeared to seven of His disciples who were fishing (Peter and John were among them). See how the Lord sought them though they returned to fishing! St. Augustine contemplates on this, saying, 'Christ appeared to Peter, not while occupied with catching souls, but while catching fish'. It is comforting to us to know that the Lord is ready to appear to us not while we are doing spiritual work, but also while we are busy with material work. It is He who starts; he appears and starts talking with us for our benefit.

* **The Lord appeared to two of the disciples who knew Him not.**

These are the two disciples from Emmaus to whom the Lord appeared though they knew Him not. Even when He asked them what they were talking about, they answered Him, *"Are You the only stranger in Jerusalem, and have You not known the things which happened there in these days?"*. Then the Lord Christ, beginning at Moses and all the prophets, expounded to them in all the Scriptures the things concerning Himself (Lk. 24: 18-27). At last their eyes were opened and they knew Him (Lk. 24: 31).

If you have not yet known Him, He is ready to appear to you and reveal Himself. He is ready to expound the things concerning Himself, making your heart inflamed within you, while He is expounding the Scriptures (Lk. 24: 33).

Even in repentance, in most cases God takes the initiative and only requires that we respond to Him.

He started with giving us the conscience and the power to discern. He gave us also His Holy Spirit to convict us of sin (Jn. 16: 8), to lead us to repentance. If we slacken, He sends us an encouraging word, an effective sermon or a useful book. Moreover the visits of grace do not leave us and lead us to repentance. God might permit that some disease or pain befalls us to awaken. He might permit a certain accident to happen to us and have its effect on us; or might move our hearts by the death of someone beloved to us. In many ways we feel God pricking our hearts that we may repent. It is important that we respond and not kick against the goads (Acts 9: 5). But could we repent by our own effort? Nay, for the Lord says:

"*Without Me you can do nothing*" (Jn. 15: 5)

We have hope then that God works in us for our salvation. Even if we do not have the will, we hope God gives us the will, as st. Paul the apostle says, *"for it is God who works in you both to will and to do for His good pleasure"* (Phil. 2: 13). So, *"work out your own salvation with fear and trembling"* (Phil. 2: 12).

When David the Prophet fell in sin he was not aware of the seriousness of his sin.

After the fall David was led from one sin to another without being aware how far he had gone until God sent him Nathan the Prophet. Nathan gave David an example that made him feel his crime, and from that time on David began a life of repentance, tears and regret which he recorded in many of his psalms. It was God who started and led David to heart contrition.

Another example is Lot in the land of Sodom

Lot chose the planted land with the sinful stumbling blocks in it. He dwelt in Sodom and moreover he gave his daughters in marriage there. But the Lord saved Lot as st. Peter tells us in his Second Epistle, *"and delivered righteous Lot, who was oppressed by the filthy conduct of the wicked (for that righteous man, dwelling among them tormented his righteous soul from day to day by seeing and hearing their lawless deeds) (2 Pet. 2: 7, 8)"*.

When the people of Sodom were taken captives, Lot did not learn the lesson; for after Abraham had saved him he returned again to Sodom! However, when God wanted to destroy the city He sent two angels to urge Lot to hurry out of the place, *"And while he lingered, the men took hold of his hand, his wife's hand, and the hands of his two daughters, the Lord being merciful to him, and they brought him out and set him outside the city"* (Gen. 19: 16). You should therefore trust that God is ready to work with you as He worked with Lot. He will bring you out of the land of sin provided that you give Him the lead and look not behind as Lot's wife had done.

Say then in your prayer: O Lord, work with me and never wait till I start, for perhaps I will never start.

Say to Him: Start with me as You had started with the others. Take me out of Sodom by the hands of Your holy angels. Let Your kind voice ring in my ears, *"Escape for your life! Do not look behind you nor stay anywhere in the plain ... lest you be destroyed*" (Gen. 19: 17).

Let us sing with the psalmist, "*Our soul has escaped as a bird from the snare of the fowlers; the snare is broken, and we have escaped. Our help is in the name of the Lord*" (Ps. 124: 7, 8).

You, Lord, have broken the snare, for a bird cannot break the snare of the fowlers.

Had Mary the Coptic ever thought of repentance? Nay, she was committing sins continually till God interfered and the miracle took place. She was awakened and led to repentance. God continued His work with her till she became a hermit. God interfered also in the life of Augustine, Pelagia and Sarah; and turned them to His way. The initiative was from God.

In the ministry, God calls, sends and grants the power of His Holy Spirit to work with us. He might also prepare everything for us, saying:

"***I sent you to reap that for which you have not labored***" **(Jn. 4: 38).**

"*Others have labored, and you have entered into their labors*" He prepares the way for us, He evin gives us the word to open our mouths (Eph. 6: 19). God also gives the impression on the listeners so that they follow what they hear. Let no one then fear to serve the word of God, but rather remember God's work in the word.

Even for the eternal life, God starts the preparation for us:

"***I go to prepare a place for you*" (Jn. 14: 2)**

Blessed is Your love, O Lord! May You prepare for us that place and take us to You that where You are, there we may be also (Jn. 14: 3)!

CHAPTER 13

The End Of A Thing Is Better Than Its Beginning

The worry and fear of the disciples on the day of the crucifixion and Golgotha ended with their joy and comfort on the day of the Resurrection. This reminds us of an important verse included in the Book of Ecclesiastes which says, *"The end of a thing is better than its beginning"* (Ecc. 7: 8). **Of course the end should be a good end**; for a good end makes one forget all one's worries and remember only that good comforting end. This happened at the Lord Christ's Resurrection, as all the sufferings of the disciples on the day of the crucifixion were abolished by the Resurrection.

People, therefore, always seek and care for the end.

In all matters, whether a story told or a film watched, we are interested in how the story ended. Likewise, in the case of a lawsuit, differences between a couple, or an accident on the road, what we are anxious about is how that ended. You may hear from someone the details of the event, but you ask anxiously: How did it end?. The same in the case of a match, a competition, a war between two countries, a dialogue or negotiation, the important question is: How did it end? Or what was the result?

Even in the spiritual life, what avails is the end. That is why st. Paul the apostle says of the men of God,

"Whose faith follow, considering the outcome of their conduct" **(Heb. 13: 7)**

The church reminds us of this fact when celebrating the saints; for the church celebrates the birthday of a very few such as st. Mary (on the first of the month Bashans), John the Baptist (30 Baouna) and Anba Shenouda the chief hermit (7 Bashans). But almost all the saints are celebrated on the day of their departure or martyrdom, that is at the end of their lives when they have completed their struggle successfully.

Some people started well but ended badly.

An example of those is Demas the disciple of st. Paul the Apostle. The apostle mentioned Demas among the pillars of the church: st. Mark, st. Luke & Aristorkhos, but finally he said about him, *"Demas has forsaken me, having loved this present world"* (2 Tim. 4: 10). St. Paul said also that many were like Demas, *"For many walk, of whom I have told you often, and now tell you even weeping, that they are the enemies of the cross of Christ: whose end is destruction ... and whose glory is in their shame"* (Phil. 3: 18, 19).

How strange that the end of those was destruction! What avails then is the end.

Many had begun in the Spirit but were made perfect by the flesh like the Galatians. Solomon the Wise also began with great wisdom but ended with the worship of idols (1 Kgs. 11). However we hope that he repented afterwards and ended virtuously forsaking all pleasures as evident from the Book of Ecclessiastes. Therefore we say *"The end of a thing is better than its beginning"*. At least this is what the divine inspiration said by the mouth of Solomon.

Stories that ended well:

The Scriptures tell us about stories that ended well, among which are the following:

* **The story of Joseph the Righteous** began with the cruelty and dishonesty of his brothers who sold him as a slave. Then he worked as a servant in the house of Potiphar where he was accused falsely and imprisoned. But the important thing was the end, when he became a father to Pharaoh (Gen. 45: 8), having full power and authority over the land of Egypt. His joy was completed when he received his father and brothers who wept before him asking his forgiveness. What a good end indeed far better than the beginning.

* **The same can be said about Daniel and the three young men.**

Daniel was cast into the den of lions, but the matter ended with God sending His angel and shutting the lions' mouths (Da. 6: 22). And the three young men were cast into the burning fiery furnace, but the end was that they saw them walking in the midst of the fire without being hurt and a fourth with them like the Son of God (Da. 3: 25). In both stories the end was the worship and glorification of the True God; a good end indeed better than the beginning!

* **Job the Righteous is another example.** He underwent a temptation beyond the power of any human, as he lost his children, his money, his health and his dignity. The temptation extended to the utmost, but what was the end? The Scriptures say, *"And the Lord restored Job's losses ... Indeed the Lord gave Job twice as much as he had before ... Now the Lord blessed the latter days of Job more than his beginning ... After this Job lived one hundred and forty years, and saw his children and grandchildren for four generations"* (Job 42: 10-17). What a good end!

Time is lacking to mention more and more stories that ended well and recorded in the Scriptures. What can we say about **offering Isaac** as a burnt offering, about **Nehemiah** building the walls of Jerusalem after being destroyed and burnt (Neh. 1) , or about those who were taken captives in Babylon and returned finally after having wept by the rivers of Babylon, hung their harps upon the willows and exclaimed how they would sing the Lord's song in a foreign land. Many are the good ends for which we say, *"The end of a thing is better than its beginning"*.

We say the same concerning the stories of the repentants

We remember st. Augustine and how he began a reckless

wanton life; st. Moses the black who started as a cruel murderer; st. Mary the Coptic, Pelagia and Sarah who began their lives as harlots but ended as great saints. Nothing can be said but that the end of a thing is better than its beginning.

One should therefore care for the end in any matter.

In any way you walk ask yourself: what is the end of this way? And in any project you plan, or relationship you establish ask the same question. Suppose that a young man falls in love with a young woman of different religion, he should think what the end of such relationship would be and what would happen in the future to them both. Or one quarrels with his wife and no peace can be reached between them, here this person should think what the end is and to what it may lead. If a person also starts smoking, even one cigarette to imitate his friends or to try smoking, he should think deeply what the end would be.

Whenever one is subject to any deed that may turn into a habit, one should ask oneself what the end may be.

Whenever one utters a word or feels angry, one should ask oneself what the end may be, what the response would be from the others, what the end of such anger would be, and what the result of such a word or behaviour would be.

Whenever you undergo a hardship, fall not in despair, nor be confused but rather say *"The end of a matter is better than its beginning"*. Say to yourself there will certainly be an end, and that end is in the hand of God the compassionate and merciful, therefore it will undoubtedly be better. You should say so not only with regard to your own problems but also with regard to any problem or hardship that befells an acquaintance or a friend of yours or even the church.

Probably the above verse occupied the minds of the martyrs and confessors

Probably they exclaimed: What is the end of suffering and death? Is not the end attaining the other world, Paradise, crowns and eternal happiness finally? No doubt this is much better. Where is then your sting, O death? It no more exists. The end of the matter is better than its beginning, and eternity, no doubt, is a better end. The other world is a better world where, *"Eye has not seen, nor ear heard, nor have entered into the heart of man the things which God has prepared for those who love Him"* (1 Cor. 2: 9). The spiritual heavenly body in which we will live after the resurrection (1 Cor. 15: 44-49) is undoubtedly better than this material body we have now. Our companionship with God and His angels and saints is incomparably better than the companionship in the present world. Our life in a world which is all good will be better than our life in this world where good and evil exist together, and so also the wheat and the tares.

Since eternity is better, why do we fear it? Why do we not get ready for it?

Probably, in times of hardships, we remember the words of Jeremiah the Prophet by which he blamed the Lord God, saying, *"Righteous are You, O Lord, when I plead with You; yet let me talk with You about Your judgments. Why does the way of the wicked prosper? Why are those happy who deal so treacherously?"* (Jer. 12: 1). But st. Augustine answers these questions in the light of the end of the matter, he says: The wicked, like smoke, rise always high, but while rising the smoke extends then vanishes whereas fire remains below but is firm and strong. One, therefore, should be concerned first about the end, no matter what trouble or hardship there might be.

A good end for a difficult beginning:

A spiritual life starts with a narrow gate and a difficult way (Mt. 7: 13, 14). However this leads to eternal happiness whereas the wide gate and broad way lead to destruction. See then the beautiful words of the psalmist:

"Those who sow in tears shall reap in joy" **(Ps. 126: 5)**

CHAPTER 14

You can do everything
No purpose of Yours
can be withheld from You

(Job 42: 2)

Marvellous indeed are God's works and reveal His incredible power. Man stands amazed before God's works and can say nothing but the words of Job the Righteous:

"I know that You can do everything, and that no purpose of Yours can be withheld from You" **(Job 42: 2)**

We read marvellous stories in the Scriptures, whether stories of help, of repentance and conversion, or of faith. One becomes astonished on reading such stories and say: who could believe such things would happen?

Who could believe?

But see the following examples:

The child Moses:

Moses was a small child born in a dark age and destined to die before being born. His parents hid him three months, and they could no longer hide him, they put him in an ark which they laid by the river's bank.

Who could believe that this child destined to die and laid in the water become God's great prophet and spokesman!

He became the Prophet Moses to whom the Law has been ascribed (Moses Law). He became the man of miracles and wonders who divided the red sea with his rod, struck the rock and the waters gushed out, and brought down manna and quails from heaven!

Who could believe that this child destined to die by the order of Pharaoh would live forty years in Pharaoh's palace as a prince and as a son to Pharaoh's daughter.

He became afterwards a mighty power dreaded by Pharaoh. Before him Pharaoh cried out *"I have sinned"* (Ex. 9: 27), and asked him to entreat the Lord on his behalf to stop the plagues.

Who could believe all that would happen to the little child cast in water? But it is God's hand which interferes and arranges. It is God to whom Job said, "*I know that You can do everything, and that no purpose of Yours can be withheld from You*"

The story of the child Moses gives us a lesson in hope, that God's power turns weakness into strength and changes the lives of people according to His good will.

Truly, God do marvellous works beyond our thinking. We see the present only, and see in it difficult complicated things that cause distress or despair. We may see also risks which one can hardly escape, but the future, which is under God's control, is very different from the present which we see and perhaps completely the opposite.

Let us in hope see the joyful future which is in God's hand instead of confining ourselves to the troublesome present in front of us.

The formless earth:

God gave us hope since the very beginning of creation, where the divine inspiration says, "*The earth was without form, and void; and darkness was on the face of the deep*" (Gen. 1: 2). The image is gloomy since the beginning, but we should not stop at this point for the story has not ended. Amidst this gloomy image there was some hope represented in the words, "*the Spirit of God was hovering over the face of the waters*". And what else? "*Then God said, 'Let there be light'; and there was light. And God saw the light, that it was good*" (Gen. 1).

See what a gate of light has opened before the gloomy image!

Everything has changed and God's hand began to work:

arranging, putting in order, creating life, regulating, and arraying with beauty and splendour. And God saw everything He had made, and indeed it was very good!

Who could have believed that the formless, void earth, covered with water and wrapped in darkness would turn into such beauty in which we live now. How beautiful is everything around us: trees, flowers, fruits, seas and rivers, birds and colorful butterflies, beautiful heaven, moon and stars, mountains, hills and lakes! What a beauty that poets sing the praise of and the artists represent in their marvellous works!

The story of nature in the beginning of its creation implies a symbol and hope for us.

It is a symbol of every formless, void and dark life that waits in hope God's word, *"Let there be light"*. This dark life waits God's hand to complete the picture as in the first six days of creation so that the end might be *"very good"*

Do not stop, brother, at the words *"without form and void"* getting depressed, but rather look forward to the future, in hope, and wait for the Lord. Whenever a day passes, as the divine inspiration says, *"So the evening and the morning were the ... day"*, rejoice from all your heart and say, *"Oh, clap your hands, all you peoples! Shout to God with the voice of triumph!"* (Ps. 46: 1). I know, O Lord, that You can do everything, and that no purpose of Yours can be withheld from You.

God is capable of changing everything to the best and to the opposite. The beginnings are not important with God, but rather the end of the matters.

The barren:

Among the beautiful verses on hope is the song of the barren woman in the Book of Isaiah:

"Sing, O barren, You have not borne! Break forth into singing, and cry aloud ... For more are the children of the desolate than the children of the married woman ... Enlarge the place of your tent, and let them stretch out the curtains of your dwellings ... For you shall expand to the right and to the left, and your descendants will inherit the nations, and make the desolate cities inhabited. Do not fear, for you will not be ashamed" (Isa. 54: 1-4).

There is hope indeed for the barren, not only to have children, but also to have her children inherit cities!

The barren woman is a symbol of the nations who were desolate and desolate from God. She is also a symbol of every sinful soul far from the communion of the Spirit and the fruit of the Spirit. There is hope for her, not only to have offspring and fruit, but rather more to enlarge the place of her tent for she will expand to the right and to the left.

You should not only have patience and hope but moreover to sing.

Rejoice in hope, and stop not at your being barren but look forward to the promise that will be fulfilled. Truly, O Lord, You can do everything, and no purpose of Yours can be withheld from You!

Stories of help:

* Who could believe that the child David would have victory over Goliath the Valiant?

David had that hope by which he said to Goliath, *"This day the Lord will deliver you into my hand"* (1 Sam. 17: 46).

But for that hope, David would not have proceeded with confidence to fight Goliath. He was not afraid at all, while all the army was in fear.

Hope made st. Mark come to Egypt as Evangelist

He had no people nor church in Egypt. There was only Pharonic, Greek and Roman worship, besides the Jewish religion, the heathen philosophy and the School of Alexandria. There prevailed the sword of the Roman Empire governing the country as well as the intrigues of the Jews.

Who could believe that the young man Mark overcome all impediments and spread faith all over Egypt? Truly God can do everything and no purpose of His can be withheld from Him. How beautiful are the words of the Scriptures here:

* *"Who are you, O great mountain? Before Zerubbabel you shall become a plain"* **(Zech. 4: 7).**

Indeed, hope makes us see everything easy.

Hope makes us see a way open amidst the sea, and hear the words of Moses the Prophet, *"The Lord will fight for you, and you shall hold your peace"* (Ex. 14: 14).

Hope makes us trust that the staff of Elisha restores to life the person on whom it is laid.

Hope makes us trust that we will enter the land even if we are lost in the wilderness for forty years.

Hope made Jonah sure that he would look again toward God's holy temple (Jon. 2: 4), so he prayed while inside the belly of the fish.

Hope protected Peter from falling into despair after his denial of the Lord.

He had hope that the Lord would forgive him and accept him again as apostle. Who could have thought that the person who had been afraid and denied the Lord in front of a servant girl would have the courage to stand before the council and the high priest and say to them, *"We ought to obey God rather than men"* (Acts 5: 29). Who could have thought that Peter suffer for the Lord, preach, and die as a martyr!

The stories of the apostles' evangelism give us lessons in hope.

"God has chosen the foolish things of the world to put to shame the wise" (1 Cor. 1: 27). These little minority were able to resist the power of the Roman Empire and the intrigues of the Jews. The words of those who had no speech nor language has gone through all the earth and to the end of the world (Ps. 19: 3, 4). In thirty four years they could spread Christianity in all Middle East, Egypt, Turkey, Greece, Rome, and in many parts of Europe, Asia and Africa. Does not this give us hope that God works in us for His kingdom?

Who could have believed that the captive Nehemiah receive enough support to reconstruct the wall of Jerusalem?

Nothing could be withheld from God. Even when Daniel was cast in the lions' den, God sent His angel and shut the lions' mouths. And when the three young men were cast into the burning fiery furnace, they were not hurt and the Son of God was walking with them in the midst of the fire (Da. 3: 25). Joseph, likewise, though cast in prison, came out to rule over Egypt.

Who could believe that Saul of Tarsus, who persecuted the church, become the greatest evangelist in Christianity and labor more abundantly than all the other apostles (1 Cor. 15: 10)?

Who could believe that Irianos the Governor of Ensena and the most cruel and harsh governor that tormented the martyrs in the reign of Diocletian, would believe and become himself a martyr? Also Longinos the soldier who struck the Lord Christ's side with the spear, believed at the end and was martyred. Really, O Lord, You can do everything, and no purpose of Yours can be withheld from You!

It is the greatest miracle worked continually by the Lord, that is changing the attitude of the people.

The stories of repentance do also give us wonderful hope, and how many they are!

Who could believe that Mary Magdalene, out of whom the Lord cast seven demons (Lk. 8: 4) would announce the event of the Resurrection to the apostles?

Who could think that Mary the Coptic, who had been a harlot, become a hermit? The same applies to Augustine, Moses the black and others.

All things are possible:

With God all things are possible (Mt. 19: 26), this is natural. But see what st. Paul the apostle says: *"I can do all things through Christ who strengthens me"* (Phil. 4: 13)! Another verse that creates hope is:

"All things are possible to him who believes" **(Mk. 9: 23)**

By this hope we get the power with which we overcome throughout our lives. On the other hand, Satan leads the people to despair, fear, hesitation and feeling of weakness and disability to paralyze them. Satan may also make them feel the cross heavy and fear the narrow gate and the difficult way so that they cannot move one step forward. Therefore, say with Paul the Apostle,

I can do all things through Christ who strengthens me

Say to yourself He who changed Saul of Tarsus can change me; He who gave Augustine repentance can make me repent; He who helped David against Goliath can help me; He who accepted the despised and those who have no existence can accept me

Hope gives the power to work and to avoid thinking of failure.

We should not think of failure at all so long as God's hand is with us. Whatever leads to despair we face with God's unlimited power and God's interference with all His love to change things to the best.

Many times God says: Fear not. Do not be afraid.

He did not allow Moses to be afraid of meeting Pharaoh (Ex. 4), nor Jeremiah of his young age. He said to Joshua the son of Nun after Moses' death, *"No man shall be able to stand before you all the days of your life ... I will not leave you nor forsake you. Be strong and of good courage ... do not be afraid, nor be dismayed, for the Lord God is with you"* (Josh. 1: 5, 9). To believe that God works with you gives you hope. Moreover, there is the very amazing promise of the Lord,

"he who believes in Me, the works that I do he will do also; and greater works than these he will do" **(Jn. 14: 12)**

What a promise, O Lord, we do not deserve! But it is Your marvellous love and your promises. We believe in Your love and your generous giving as well as your interference for help. We believe also that the battle is the Lord's (1 Sam. 17: 47), and that nothing restrains the Lord from saving by many or be few (1 Sam. 14: 6)

God is able to win by Joshua's army, and able to win by David's stone!

Even though you are weak or young, God is able to work in you and with you as He had done with Jeremiah the child and David the lad. He had done so also with Samuel the child to reproach through him Eli the high priest (1 Sam. 3: 10-18).

Since the battle is the Lord's, you have to depend on Him and to put your hope in Him even though you are hindered by some sin or lust, some temptation or hardship, and even though the wicked people resist you. Remember the stories of the men of God who out of weakness were made strong (Heb. 11: 33, 34), and who became valiant in battle and subdued kingdoms.

Those were the truly mighty men who feared nothing.

Do not weaken nor be shaken by temptations, troubles, sins, lusts or enemies. Be as the house built on the rock which does not fall by any rain or wind (Mt. 7: 25). Be like the gandola in the River Nile which waters cannot overcome.

Put before you some verses that give you comfort and strength

"Yea, though I walk through the valley of the shadow of death, I will fear no evil; for You are with me" (Ps. 23: 4).

"Though an army may encamp against me, my heart shall not fear; Though war may rise against me, in this I will be confident." (Ps. 27: 3)

"Many a time they have afflicted me from my youth; yet they have not prevailed against me ... The Lord is righteous; He has cut in pieces the cords of the wicked" (Ps. 129: 2, 4).

"The snare is broken, and we have escaped. Our help is in the name of the Lord" (Ps. 124: 7, 8)

"You pushed me violently, that I might fall, but the Lord helped me. The Lord is my strength ..." (Ps. 118: 13, 14)

Remember the history of the saints who never feared and never failed.

CHAPTER 15

Behold, a door standing Open in heaven

The Book of Revelation is recorded by st. John the Beloved, and starts with the words, *"I, John, both your brother and companion in the tribulation and kingdom and patience of Jesus Christ"*. **St. John said this phrase when he was exiled on the island called Patmos.** In spite of being away from any human help or comfort, the divine consolations did not leave him. St. John saw the Lord on that island and received messages from Him. See what he says, *"After these things I looked, and behold, a door standing open in heaven ... and behold, a throne set in heaven ..."* (Rev. 4: 1, 2). What an amazing comfort to this great apostle in his tribulation and exile! It reminds us of the words of the Lord to the angel of the Church in Philadelphia:

"See, I have set before you an open door, and none can shut it" **(Rev. 3: 8)**

It is the promise of God who opens and no one shuts, and shuts and no one opens (Rev. 3: 7). It is a word of comfort which whenever we remember, we are filled with hope and rejoice in that heavenly open door.

Truly, when all doors are shut, God's door remains open and no one can shut it.

For this, one should always be in peace even though all doors are shut, because God the compassionate can open and no one shuts. This makes God's children live in complete happiness and no outer pressing circumstances can shake their trust.

The Scriptures give us the example of David the prophet while pursued by King Saul:

Saul, with all his authority, his cruelty, his craftiness and his hatred to David, pursued him in the wilderness from one cave to the other intending to kill him and plotting against him. But in spite of all this God protected David and saved him whereas King Saul died without doing him harm.

Even Absalom, with all his treachery, could not harm David.

The reason is that God opened a door before David through which he could attain glory remembering the many experiences he underwent as the enemies arose against him. He once said, "*Lord, how they have increased who trouble me! Many are they who rise up against me. Many are they who say of me, 'There is no help for him in God'*" (Ps. 3: 1, 2). He said also, "***Those who hate me without a cause are more than the hairs of my head***" (Ps. 69: 4). If we ask David the Prophet: What did you do for those? Did they destroy you? He will answer us: The Lord was a shield for me, my glory who lift up my head, "*I cried to the Lord with my voice, and He heard me from His holy hill*" (Ps. 3: 3, 4). "*I looked, and behold, a door standing open in heaven*". The many who rose against David could not shut the door which the Lord opened before him. Does not this story give you a spiritual rule; that is:

Your life is in God's hand not in the people's.

When Esau said, "*I will kill my brother Jacob*" (Gen. 27: 41), he could not do that because Jacob saw a door standing open in heaven, and a ladder set up on the earth and its top reaching to heaven with the angels of God ascending and descending on it (Gen. 28: 12). The result was that on Jacob's return, "*Esau ran to meet him, and embraced him, and fell on his neck and kissed him, and they wept*" (Gen. 33: 4).

Indeed God can change situations and change the hearts

It is truly written, "*When a man's ways please the Lord, He makes even his enemies to be at peace with him*" (Prov. 16: 7). Even if the enemies do not be at peace with a person, they will not prevail against him as the Lord said to Jeremiah the Prophet, "*They will fight against you, but they shall not prevail against you. For I am with you, to deliver you"* (Jer. 1: 19).

Many were those who rose against Christ's disciples and apostles!

The scribes, the Pharisees, the Sadducees, the priests and chief priests of the Jews, the elders, the Roman governors and rulers, all those arose against the disciples and apostles of the Lord, cast them in prison and scourged them. But God had set before them a door open, thus their preaching extended everywhere, *"There is no speech nor language where their voice is not heard. Their line has gone out through all the earth"* (Ps. 19: 3, 4). Even *"those who were scattered went everywhere preaching the word"* (Acts 8: 4). When all doors were shut in front of them, God's door was open, and this was enough. Therefore, our advice to anyone undergoing troubles, tribulations or hardships:

Do not look at the shut doors, but rather to the key in God's hand.

God can *"open and no one shuts"*. He is almighty, and He loves you and loves good for you. All those who rise against you have limited power, because they are human beings. Even Satan's power is limited because he is created. God alone is unlimited and His power is limitless.

God, the Unlimited, therefore said to Paul the Apostle, *"My grace is sufficient for you"* **(2 Cor. 12: 9).**

It is God's grace that can open for you a way in the sea (Ex. 14) and bring you water from the rock (Ex. 17: 6) or destroy mountains before you. God said of His help to His servant Zerubbabel, *"Who are you, O great mountain? Before Zerubbabel you shall become a plain"* (Zech. 4: 7).

Time is lacking if we want to tell stories of saints experiencing God's open door.

Is it enough to speak about **st. Athanasius the Apostolic** to whom people said: [The whole world is against you, Athanasius], yet he stood against the heretic world at that time and prevailed because God opened a door before him? Or should we speak about **Nehemiah** for whom God opened a wonderful door, and behold a heathen king provide him with all provisions to rebuild Jerusalem, and he turned from a captive to a ruler in the city of God?

This is also **Eliezer of Damascus** whom God guided to Rebekah to take her as wife to Isaac his master's son through marvellous divine guidance! Eliezer felt this help and said, *"Do not hinder me, since the Lord has prospered my way"* (Gen. 24: 56).

Many also are the doors open for repentance.

Who could imagine that a door of repentance would be open before Mary the Coptic through whom hundreds stumbled and fell! But God did open a door for her through a miracle by which she felt God's hand and repented.

Who could imagine that a door would be open before Augustine, Pelagia, and Moses the black after they had reached such a bad condition far from God!

See also Saul of Tarsus the persecutor of the church.

Who could believe that Saul of Tarsus would become an apostle and a chosen vessel of the Lord after breathing threats and bringing men and women bound to prison (Acts 9: 1, 2)! But a door in heaven opened before him while on his way to Damascus through an amazing vision where the Lord talked to him. Finally Saul believed and turned to the opposite, endured labors more abundantly than all the other apostles, and obtained the crown of martyrdom.

Even the Gentiles had a door opened to them by God for repentance and acceptance.

The Gentiles were considered aliens and strangers from the covenants and promise, but they became the new olive tree that became a partaker of the root and fatness of the old olive tree. Moreover, most of the believers came out of those Gentiles and the door opened before Cornelius through a miracle (Acts 10), then before all the others (Acts 15).

Many are the wonderful examples praised in the Scriptures:

Among these examples are: the widow of Zarephath which belongs to Sidon who provided for him; the Canaanite woman whose daughter the Lord Christ healed; Rahab the harlot; Ruth; the queen of Sheba who came from the ends of the earth to hear the wisdom of Solomon, and all those whose names have been recorded in the history and were praised just because God opened a door before each of them.

What can be said about Jonah the Prophet who was swallowed by the fish?

Who could believe that Jonah would come out of the belly of the fish, live, and preach Nineveh and that Nineveh would believe through him? It is the door which God opened before him that made the fish open its mouth and cast him on the shore to perform the mission entrusted to him!! True indeed are the words of the Gospel:

"The things which are impossible with men are possible with God" **(Lk. 18: 27)**

God is Almighty, if you rely on Him you will have steadfast hope which never shakes. He is able to open the shut doors and solve all complicated problems. He has in His hand all the keys *"He opens and no one shuts"*. An outstanding example of a closed door which God opened is the door of Paradise.

The Lord opened the door of Paradise after thousands of years.

He brought Adam and Eve into Paradise after being dismissed from there. He brought in all those who departed in hope, and let the door open before the thief on His right and moreover before all the repentants so that they all would rejoice in hope (Rom. 12: 12)

Ask the Lord then to open the doors before you.

Before you come out of your home everyday, ask the Lord to open before you all the hearts and the ears, and to open before you the doors of fortune and prosperity. What a beautiful prayer that which the priest says in front of the sanctuary! He says: **Let the door of Your house open before use all the days.** And also: Shut not the door of Your house in our faces. Everyday each of us prays, "*O Lord, open my lips, and my mouth shall show forth your praise*" (Ps. 51: 15). We say this because we are not sure if we open our mouths by ourselves what words we shall utter, will our words be pleasing to God or not? What will they lead to?

One of the strange prayers which Elisha prayed for his disciple Gehazi was: "***Lord, I pray, open his eyes that he might see***" (2 Kgs. 6: 17). Let him see that those who are with us are more than those who are with them, and thus he calms down and believes. Indeed, we have eyes but they cannot see, and we have ears but cannot hear. We need the Lord to open our eyes, our ears, and our hearts also as we say in our prayers, "*Open my eyes, that I may see wondrous things from Your law*" (Ps. 119: 18)

But is this all that God opens before us? Certainly not. There is much more to be said which has no place here, for God says:

"And try Me now in this, if I will open for you the windows of heaven and pour out for you such blessing that there will not be room enough to receive it"

God's door is always open for us even though all other doors are shut.

He says to the angel of the church in Philadelphia, *"See, I have set before you an open door, and no one can shut it"* (Rev. 3: 8). It is God's kind heart that removed the restraining veil and opened the way to the holy of holies and the door of Paradise before Adam and his children.

It is a comforting word we should remember at the beginning of the year.

Whenever the world seems narrow before you and everything is complicated, whenever people shut their hearts against you, and whenever you call and get no response or seek and find no friend, repeat the comforting words of st. John the Beloved, *"I looked, and behold a door standing open in heaven"*

These words are said to everyone in trouble, and to every sinner suffering from sin.

They are said to every sinner subjected to sin, who tried many times to get rid of it but could not and is falling in despair. They are said to that sinner who tried the door of spiritual exercises and struggling, and knocked at the doors of fasting and self-control but could not find the door of repentance open before him.

Let that sinner lift his eyes upward and say *"behold, a door standing open in heaven"* *"My help comes from the Lord, who made heaven and earth"* (Ps. 121: 2).

It is important to lift our eyes high towards heaven to see the open door and get comfort.

The problem is that in our troubles we seek worldly help! We use our intellect and power, and seek the help of the people. We try any possibilities and circumstances, thus we fall in confusion, anxiety and disturbance. But if we lift our sight upwards and see the open door in heaven, all this will vanish and we will be at rest. Let us do as st. John the Beloved, our companion in the tribulation, had done.

Notice that st. John saw the open door without asking for that. The door did not even open by his prayers, but it was open by itself, through the divine love.

St. John did not say: May You open for me a door in heaven that I might see Your throne and Your heavenly hosts. But God showed John all this out of His kindness, that he might know how God's gifts are due to His love and His goodness. To those in trouble God says *"Knock, and it will be opened to you"* (Mt. 7: 7; Lk. 11: 9), but to those who live in faith He says, *"all these things shall be added to you"* (Mt. 6: 33). The things you need will be given you from the heavenly Father who loves His children and knows their needs without their asking.

That door God opens and no one can shut.

According to His faithful promise, *"He opens and no one shuts"* (Rev. 3: 7). Whenever He opens a door before you, all matters will be easy for you, *"No man shall be able to stand before you"* (Josh. 1: 5); *"no one will attack you to hurt you"* (Acts 18: 10); the gates of Hades shall not prevail against you (Mt. 16: 18). Do not waste your time then hewing broken cisterns that can hold no water (Jer. 2: 13), but rely on the divine help that guarantees you an open door in heaven. Then you will have everything.

This open door John saw in his tribulation, while exiled in the island called Patmos, persecuted for the word of God.

He saw this open door when he could find no mercy or justice in the world, no help or support from anyone, but all had forsaken him or at least could offer him no help. He was left to his enemies to judge him. And while all the doors on the earth were shut, he looked, and behold a door was standing open in heaven. Then he heard a voice saying, *"Come up here, and I will show you"*, and he saw God's throne and the heavenly hosts in the vision.

How marvellous God is in His gifts! He raises the poor out of the dust (Ps. 113: 7)

Probably st. John said to the Lord: Who am I, O Lord, that You do all this to me. I am poor and cast on this remote island; I do not deserve to see even the throne of Emperor Trajan, how far more undeserving to see the throne of the king of kings and Lord of lords?! But the Lord asserted: Come up, John, to see that Throne, to know that all the emperors of the world are mere handful of dust! But let us see:

How did John go up into heaven to see that vision?

Language fails to give an answer. Yea, no answer can be given. Neither the Arabic language, nor any other language contains terms that can express what has happened. It is left to your own contemplations.

"Come up here", how did John comply to this order?, or rather how was the order completed for John? How did John go up into heaven? How did he enter through that open door? How did he see, is it with the spirit or with a spiritual eye, or otherwise? The important thing is that God turned his tribulation into joy, his ignorance into knowledge, his exile into elevation

and grace, and to us God gave the promise of another life after resurrection and hope in this life.

All these things happened to John while in exile!

This revelation did not come to John while he was in Jerusalem the city of the Great King, or while in the Temple, in the Holy of Holies, beside the Ark of Covenant, nor in any of those great holy places where such revelations can be expected. On the contrary the revelation came to John while in tribulation and during exile.

Truly, the kingdom of God does not come with observation (Lk. 17: 20).

We do not know when or where will God's grace visit us through the work of His Holy Spirit. We do not know when heaven would open its doors, or when will the voice come to us as a sound of trumpet, a stormy wind, or as many waters? God does not visit us while we are waiting, or when we expect or observe. We do not know when he will come to help us or when He will reveal Himself to us.

We should then be ready to receive the work of the Spirit within us. We should open our hearts and God will open for us a door in heaven.

We should lift our spirits to heaven while our bodies are on the earth. In this way the Lord will lift us to heaven even though we remain in the flesh on the earth as the apostle says, *"whether in the body ... or whether out of the body I do not know, God knows"* (2 Cor. 12: 3).

The greatest hope in which we rejoice which the Revelation of John has brought us is that:

The doors of heaven have become open, and st. Stephen had seen that before.

When the Jews gnashed with their teeth at st. Stephen to kill him, *"he, being full of the Holy Spirit, gazed into heaven and saw the glory of God, and Jesus standing at the right hand of God, and said, 'Look! I see the heavens opened and the Son of Man standing at the right hand of God!'"* (Acts 7: 55, 56).

This opened heaven is our great hope which we seek to see the glory of God and the Lord Christ in it

St. Stephen the archdeacon and st. John the Beloved saw this opened heaven. They saw also part of the forthcoming glory as a guarantee of the eternal kingdom. The amazing thing is that each of them saw the open heaven while he was suffering, persecuted and forsaken by people. One of them saw that vision while being stoned, and the other while in exile. The purpose is to make us understand that the way to this heaven is the Cross, and that *"we must through many tribulations enter the kingdom of God"* (Acts 14: 22)

Before Stephen and John, Ezekiel the Prophet had seen that opened heaven.

Ezekiel saw the throne of God carried by the Cherubim (Ezek. 1). He saw this scene when he was among the captives by the River Chebar, as he said, *"Now it came to pass ... as I was among the captives by the River Chebar, that the heavens were opened and I saw visions of God ..."*, and after describing what he had seen, he said, *"This was the appearance of the likeness of the glory of the Lord. So when I saw it, I fell on my face, and I heard a voice of One speaking"* (Ezek. 1: 28). How strange it is that he saw the vision while in captivity, as John saw the revelation while in exile!

Daniel the Prophet also saw a similar scene while in captivity.

. Daniel saw the Son of Man coming with the clouds of

heaven before the Father, and He was given dominion and glory and a kingdom that all peoples, nations, and languages should serve Him, "*His dominion is an everlasting dominion, which shall not pass away, and His kingdom the one which shall not be destroyed*" (Da. 7: 13, 14). Daniel saw another vision and God sent him Gabriel the angel to make him understand the vision (Da. 8: 16).

All those visions have been revealed to prophets and saints in tribulations.

As we have seen, the heaven and the throne of God John saw while in exile, and Stephen while being stoned, whereas Ezekiel and Daniel saw them while being in captivity. No doubt such scenes which God permits His saints to see in their tribulations for His name are a kind of divine comfort for them while suffering.

What about you, brethren? Have you seen this opened heaven, or you have eyes but cannot see?

If our eyes cannot see, when will the veil be removed that we may see what the spirituals can see. While in the body we cannot see, but when we become in the Spirit as John was in the Spirit on the Lord's Day (Rev. 1: 10), then we will see.

So long as our eyes are occupied with the flesh, the material and the world, and so long as our eyes are closed by materiality, they can never see spiritual matters.

The open heaven was seen by the saints in their tribulations but those living in luxury, enjoyment, happiness and pleasure do not feel any need to an open door in heaven! Even if those plead to God, they will say: Open for us doors on the earth. The time has not yet come for heaven. Open for us the doors of treasures, wealth and positions. I fear that those living in luxury will hear also in heaven that fearful phrase, "*Assuredly, I say to you, they have their reward"* (Mt. 6: 5)

Those who are occupied with worldly things, like those living in luxury, do not seek a door in heaven.

The thoughts of such people are concentrated in the world and in earthly matters. They have no time nor desire to lift their eyes upwards, like the foolish rich man who said, *"I will pull down my barns and build greater, and there I will store all my crops and my goods. And I will say to my soul, 'Soul you have many goods laid up for many years; take your ease; eat, drink, and be merry"* (Lk. 12: 18, 19)

We have then to go beyond the worldly matters to be able to see the open heavenly door.

Noah's ark is a good example of this. Noah came out of the world and rose above the waters that covered everything. Noah opened a window in the ark similar to the door open in heaven, and out of that window came out a dove and brought an olive leaf as symbol of the divine peace in the new land which the Lord blessed.

If you cannot go beyond earthly matters all the time, let that be for some time at least, let it be on the Lord's Day for example.

The Lord gave you that Day so that you might spend it with Him, learning earthly matters and uniting with the One i.e. God. On that Day you can think of Him, talk to Him, listen to His voice in your heart, and in short your mind gets purified -even temporarily- from all material things. Only then you will see that door.

***

✢

ENGLISH TRANSLATIONS OF BOOKS BY HIS HOLINESS POPE SHENOUDA III

Among 100 books written by His Holiness Pope Shenouda III in Arabic Language 43 have been translated into English they are :

1. Release of the Spirit.
2. Words of Spiritual Benefit. (Vol. 1).
3. Words of Spiritual Benefit. (Vol. 2).
4. Words of Spiritual Benefit. (Vol. 3).
5. Words of Spiritual Benefit. (Vol. 4).
6. Contemplations on the Ten Commandments (Vol. 1).
7. Contemplations on the Ten Commandments. (Vol. 2).
8. Contemplations on the Ten Commandments. (Vol. 3).
9. Contemplations on the Ten Commandments. (Vol. 4).
10. Contemplations on the Sermon on the Mount.
11. The Seven Words of Our Lord on the Cross.
12. Thine is the Power and the Glory.
13. Contemplations on Jonah the prophet.
14. Priesthood.
15. Salvation in the Orthodox Concept.
16. The Heresy of "Salvation in a moment".
17. Diabolic wars.
18. Spiritual warfares.
19. Lord, how ? .
20. Discipleship.

21. The Holy Zeal.
22. Being with God.
23. Lif of Faith .
24. The Creed.
25. Return to God .
26. So Many Years With the Problems of People. (Vol. 1).
27. So Many Years With the Problems of People. (Vol. 2).
28. So Many Years With the Problems of People. (Vol. 3).
29. So Many Years With the Problems of People. (Vol. 4).
30. The Spirituality of Fasting .
31. Calmness.
32. Characteristics of the Spiritual Path.
33. Experiences in life.
34. Divinity of Christ.
35. Comparative Theology .
36. The Nature of Christ .
37. Contemplations on the Resurrection.
38. The Holy Spirit and His Work in us.
39. Judge Not Others.
40. Ten Concepts.
41. Quizzes on The Holy Bible.
42. What is Man ?.
43. Matin Prayer.

www.ingramcontent.com/pod-product-compliance
Lightning Source LLC
Chambersburg PA
CBHW060747050426
42449CB00008B/1312